A Journey of Light in the Darkness

By Sister Judith Fenyvesi
of the Sisters of Social Service

Cover design by Jon Valerio

Published by
Manzella Trade Communications, Inc.
PO Box 1188, Williamsville, NY 14231-1188 U.S.A.
Telephone 716.681.8880, Fax 716.681.5678
Email Info@ManzellaTrade.com.

ISBN: 0-926566-04-0

Library of Congress Control Number: 2002115251

What reviewers are saying about
A Journey of Light in the Darkness:

"This is an unforgettably inspiring story of a gifted woman touched by God. The spirit of this extraordinary woman bridges the realities of Jews and Christians… and conservative Catholics defending the inheritance and Vatican II Catholics open to God's call for the new. Sister Judith transcends each category. Hope and love light the way through the darkness of her life-giving journey."
— Gregory Baum, Ph.D., Author of *The Twentieth Century: A Theological Overview* and Editor of *The Ecumenist* since 1963

"In India, the nature of saintliness is conveyed through a lovely, ancient metaphor: When a sandalwood tree is cut down, each blow of the axe fills the forest with fragrance. Just so, when a man or woman of God encounters sorrow or loss, each blow seems to release in them deeper reserves of love and compassion. That comparison seems… to describe very aptly the life of Sister Judith… in this exceedingly humble, yet luminous oral history."
— Carol Lee Flinders, Ph.D., Author of *Enduring Grace* and *At the Root of This Longing*

"It is stories that hold the world together and stories that break your heart wide open. Stories give hope and make you amazed that one person could have so much courage, so much forgiveness, so much love. This is such a story! Read it and be blessed."
— Sister Macrina Wiederkehr, Author of *Gold in Your Memories* and *Seasons of Your Heart*

"The Bible is really a series of short biographies, because human lives and stories touch and change us much more than mere concepts or theories. Sister Judith Fenyvesi's contemporary and challenging oral history will both touch and change you forever. It says, in effect, that true faith is 'ever ancient and ever new.' Sister Judith's life is faith become flesh."
— Father Richard Rohr, O.F.M., Author of *Everything Belongs* and *Hope Against Darkness*

The Sisters of Social Service (SSS) is an international community which was founded in 1923 in Hungary by Sister Margaret Slachta. The members of the SSS Federation live and minister to God's people in nine countries on three continents. In their Constitution, the SSS declare their mission and charism with these words: "We participate in the social mission of the Church, which we see as embracing the many needs of society arising from social, religious, economic, environmental, cultural, and civic conditions. Our call is to live a life that is rooted in the Holy Spirit, grounded in the spirit of Saint Benedict, and characterized by an informed social consciousness and contemporary lifestyle."

To honor
My mother and father,
Elizabeth and Francis Fenyvesi,
My sisters and grandmother,
And all victims of persecution.

Taken from the chorus of the play, *Judith* by Evelyn McLean Brady

Elizabeth, Mother
A shekina was Elizabeth, a woman of light.
She was a mother who made all things right.
Her brightness shone to all she'd meet.
She was the light of her home, a lamp on the street.
She always treasured motherhood's worth.
She even gave one daughter…a second birth.

Francis, Father
And when the Nazi boot was heard in our land,
Francis planned escape for many…with an open hand.
Searching every avenue for his family to leave,
Each effort was thwarted; each attempt he grieved.
When he knew hope dimmed…it broke his heart.
A father dies; her hero departs.
May he find peace from the God above,
This gentle father whose power was love.

Marianne
She carried the first of our next generation;
The first was the last; she had no protection.
I dream of my sister, I dream of her child,
How her sacred trust has been defiled.
How many mothers have stood at this cross
Their suffering and ours, the children we've lost.
Yet I know in the nightmares,
I know in the dreaming
There is in God's plan a truth, and a meaning.

Marta
Think of the air that is pure and free.
That is how Marta will always be.
Think of spring gardens ready to bloom
The fragrance of her youthful perfume.
Think of the first robin's seductive song
Think of how this young woman longed
To be a mother, to be Paul's wife
To create a home, to create her life.
Her dreams were simple, her dreams were true
Her dreams are the dreams for me and you.

Acknowledgments

This book would not be possible without the help of many people along the way. I owe much gratitude to a friend and writer, Joan Albarella. In 1990, she encouraged me to write my memoirs and then, through many hours together, recorded the oral history of my life from birth to my immigration to the U.S.

In 1994, Evelyn Brady, a dear friend, teacher and poet, thought that my oral history and life story would inspire some of her students. With the encouragement of Joan Albarella, Evelyn expanded the original version to include my life and work in the U.S.

Sister Angela Szabo, SSS, realized the potential value of having some of our history and work chronicled for our community. She encouraged and supported me in every way possible as I faced the great challenge of remembering and composing the history we all share. All of this was a highly enriching experience for me.

Later, another friend, Lisa Monagle, joined the project and helped with the completion of the book. Her interest and commitment were a source of encouragement and comfort for me. In the last year, Joan Albarella joined us again, enriching the process further with her own writing, editing and publishing experience.

Many other friends have accompanied me on this book's journey. Sister Virginia Fabili, a member of the Los Angeles Community of the Sisters of Social Service, was the first to urge me to record my life story. Caryl Fonda and her husband, Amadeo Qualish, and Lisa Murray-Roselli were invaluable editors and supporters of this project. Also, I am deeply indebted to Judy Fitzgerald Dolan, Carol Weissert, Karen A. Whitney, and Shirley Banko for their encouragement, work and advisement. I also wish to thank Donna Manzella-Dailey, James Manzella and Anthony Manzella Jr. for their assistance, as well as the members of the Advisory Board of the Sisters of Social Service for their various contributions. And lastly, I wish to thank John Manzella and Karla D. Manzella, who helped with the book's final preparation and publication.

I find no words to adequately express my gratitude for the help, support, and hard work these friends have devoted to this project. What started as an oral history evolved, for me personally, into an honest sharing of the search for my own identity along with the relationship between Judaism and the Catholic Church. It also has been a way of giving thanks for all the blessings of my life and for all the experiences of the Spirit's presence to me. And finally, it is expression of my hope for the future.

There are several organizations devoted to justice and compassion that over the years have energized and sustained my work and me. As always, the Sisters of Social Service, through their spirituality and commitment to justice, continue to encourage and inspire me. Network, the Center of Concern, and LCWR are important resources whose vision I share. The Sisters of Our Lady of Sion, the Maryknoll Sisters and the Benedictines of Erie, Pennsylvania all contributed to strengthening my understanding of and longing for a new day of peace, compassion and unity.

Finally, the profound and selfless love of my mother, Elizabeth, and my father, Francis Fenyvesi has been my most constant and faithful companion.

Foreword

The story of Sister Judith Fenyvesi is a powerful one. However, it does not come with a soundtrack or enhanced with a film director's dramatic vision. It is not accompanied by the plaintive strains of impassioned violins and keen angles of focus to tell you what to feel and where to look. The absence of such accompaniment, in the literary sense, may initially serve to lull the reader into thinking this story is an ordinary tale of an ordinary life, no more than dates and events following dates and events. The reader may find him/herself searching for the emotional tale that must be coursing through these events, for some sweeping pathos to carry her into the heart of the story, but will find only subtle hints.

This lack of emotional coloring is not a literary shortcoming, but a reflection of who Sister Judith is as a person of faith. She says, "I was…called to give my life for my loved ones, and all the victims of the world, by offering my life in ways in which their lives would be honored and values sustained." The story does not gloss over her suffering nor dismiss it as inconsequential; her suffering is simply a matter of fact, something from which she learned and by which she was able to get closer to God and to understanding her purpose in life. Suffering should bring one closer to God, closer to the full expression of oneself as love. Sister Judith speaks about the oppression of her people under the Nazis and the Soviets, her ten years in prison, her subsequent release and difficulties as an ex-prisoner in an unwelcoming Communist world, and her loneliness and struggles in the new world of the United States, but she shows us a mere glimpse into the day-to-day internal struggles that she experienced.

Upon finishing this tale, one realizes that, for Sister Judith, this story is not about the exploration of suffering, but the profound and enlightened result of it. This is a woman who has dedicated her life to the service of others…and to work. This sort of dedication has taken a toll on her health, as you will read, but this is not her concern. What comes through in the end is a life of fierce commitment to spiritual growth and to pushing against the walls of oppression. She has done so without any noticeable regard for her own well-being. Emotional indulgence would be inappropriate because the point is not to make the reader suffer with her, but to see, with a dry eye, the power of the brutality of the world and, conversely, the power of service and love.

When I first learned of Sister Judith's imprisonment, I asked her how she managed to survive so many years. She answered in her peaceful and direct way, telling me that there were many beautiful people in those prisons; they helped one another through it. She added that many people were worse off than she.

While one can be certain that there is another story inside Sister Judith's heart, one of intense personal pain, she does not think we need to know that story. Focusing on gritty details and telling us how to feel about her circumstances would take away from the simplicity and truth that drive this saga.

Sister Judith's direct delivery tells us that there are struggles, but you must concentrate on what is important, on what you can learn, on what you think you will do when the struggle is over, and how you will continue to create meaning in your life. That's it. Living is about service through work, finding your spiritual path, and love, above all, love. Sister Judith explains her ultimate goal in this way — "I live my life hoping, in some way, to contribute toward a better future for humanity, a future with justice for all."

Lisa Murray-Roselli

Chapter One

"My dear little Jutka…We can't help it, but God created you in this way."

I was born Kathleen Judith Fenyvesi on June 8, 1923 in a town called Salonta, Romania. During the years of 1940-1945, this town, along with the northern part of Transylvania, was annexed to Hungary. However, by the end of World War II, it was given back to Romania.

Salonta was located in an agricultural region, yet it resembled a small city more than a village. There was a larger city, Nagyvarad (Oradea in Romanian), about forty minutes away. There were also several little villages in between them. Today, they have been combined into one metropolitan area.

Originally, both sets of my grandparents and their families lived in Nagyvarad. My father, Francis Fenyvesi, was born there on November 2, 1890. I think he was a teenager when my grandfather Fenyvesi died.

My mother, Elizabeth Waldmann, also was born in Nagyvarad, on December 23, 1894. She had three brothers, one who died at an early age.

Grandfather Fenyvesi was a businessman and grandfather Waldmann was a lawyer. Both sets of my grandparents were Jewish. All I really know about the history of my ancestors is that my great grandfather, on my father's side of the family, was a rabbi. I'm not sure when the family came to Hungary, but they most likely came from Germany, as their last names seem to indicate. At some point, my father's family changed their name from Teitelbaum to Fenyvesi. It was very common for people in those days, who wanted to be assimilated into a new culture, to change their names. On my mother's side, my Uncle Geza changed his name from Waldmann to the Hungarian Szilagyi.

My father's mother, Jeny Fenyvesi Szabo, was widowed twice. She moved to Salonta when she married her second husband, who was a pharmacist. The reason my father came to Salonta after his studies at the university was to take over this pharmacy. My grandmother lived close to us. She was the only grandparent I knew. All the others died before I came to know them. My grandmother had three sons from her first marriage: Alexander, my father Francis, and Emeric. Her second marriage produced a fourth son, Julius.

Most of my relatives continued to live in Nagyvarad. My uncles and cousins were a constant part of our family life. It was clear that my parents' roots were there, and since we lived close by, we frequently visited with our relatives. I remember them as lovely people, intelligent and interesting.

Three of my uncles married women from Budapest and established themselves there. Two became businessmen and the other a diplomat. My uncle, Geza Szilagyi, served as a Consul of Hungary to Yugloslavia.

As I grew up, I learned that Geza had become Catholic, and Emeric had become Protestant, probably soon after World War I. I think that their decisions might have been motivated by the realization that, as Jews, their career goals could not be easily achieved. Their children were raised in the Catholic and Protestant faiths, respectively. My third uncle, Alexander Waldmann, also became Catholic, but this happened much later, in the early 1940s.

Our family kept in close contact with those living in Budapest through mutual visits. The border separated us but did not prevent us from keeping in touch, or from being a part of each other's lives. I had three cousins on my mother's side: Lillian, George and Evelyn, and three cousins on my father's side of the family: George, John and Stephen. Only one cousin is still in contact with me today – Evelyn Domjan, who also lives in the United States.

When I was growing up, the population of Salonta was primarily Hungarian. Most of the people were Protestant, but there also were some Catholics, as well as a small Jewish community. I remember the town containing a large Protestant church, a smaller Catholic church and a Jewish synagogue. As more Romanians moved into the area, a Greek Orthodox Church also was built.

The majority of the people were engaged in agricultural work or small businesses. The Jewish people were mostly professionals: doctors, lawyers and business people. We were connected socially with these professionals.

My father attended the Catholic Gymnasium in Nagyvarad and then studied in Budapest to become a pharmacist. He obtained his diploma in 1911, and then took over the pharmacy in Salonta.

An early memory of my father is of his being very committed to his work. He was so conscientious. I would see him in the pharmacy serving the customers, and I learned that he would never refuse to give medicine to people who did not have the money to pay for it. For that reason, there were always countless debtors. He also was very gentle and reverential to people, especially the peasants who would come on Fridays from the neighboring villages. Most of them were Romanian, and although he did not speak their language very well, he learned enough to communicate with them. He also was good to his employees, the pharmacy interns and the women working in the laboratory.

However, he had broader interests. If he had not been asked to take over the pharmacy from his stepfather, I think he would have become a philosopher. He was a pharmacist, but it was never enough for him. He was very gifted in mathematics. I remember him helping me with this subject throughout my years of school. He had artistic talent and painted pictures, too. I remember a picture he painted that hung in his office. It was a still life of a bowl of fruit.

His favorite hobby was playing cards, especially Rummy, which he did with some friends in the nearby coffeehouse. He was very friendly and maintained good relationships with many people in the town. His office was a favorite meeting place for doctors and other professionals, Jews and non-Jews, and Hungarians and Romanians.

As a child, I helped out in the pharmacy, especially on Fridays, market day, when it was full of people. I learned to give certain items to the customers, and I was so proud that I was able to do this. I think my father was happy to have me there. On Sunday, the pharmacy was closed, but people came to our door. The pharmacy was part of the house that we lived in. I would answer the door and ask my father where the needed item was, and then I would get it for the customer.

My mother completed school in Nagyvarad and studied at the Conservatory of Budapest. She earned her diploma in 1918 in Canto, in voice and piano. She spoke French very well, having spent some time studying in France. She also spoke German.

My parents married on March 28, 1919. This was the same day on which my father died twenty-three years later. They had three children: Marianne, born September 6, 1921; myself, born twenty months later on June 8, 1923; and Marta, born June 11, 1924, one year after me.

An early memory of my mother is of her gathering us, her three children, around the piano and teaching us beautiful songs. What a joy that was! We were very little, and she wanted to teach us to sing. I remember standing near the piano. She would play and she would teach us songs. She had all these books of children's songs in Hungarian that she had

3

brought from Budapest. We had a lovely time.

Later, she started to teach us to play the piano and to speak a little French. When I went to high school, I never had time to practice the piano because there was so much homework, so I gave it up. I have always regretted that, but at least I have inherited a love of music.

I also had great admiration for my mother's social skills. She was very relaxed and comfortable with company, a perfect hostess who knew how to relate to everyone. She was a wonderful role model: able to integrate the roles of mother, wife and friend. As the youngest in her family, she also was a favorite of her brothers.

My mother was a dedicated teacher, as well. She was asked to teach French and music in the middle school in Salonta. There wasn't anyone else in the town who could do it. She also gave private piano lessons in our home.

Her hobbies included sports, especially tennis, swimming, ice-skating, and hiking. She introduced us to these things early in life. She not only taught us to sing and to speak French, but also to enjoy nature.

My mother kept a diary of our childhood. After she and my sisters were taken away by the Nazis, a neighbor kept the diary and some photographs for me. I am so grateful that by almost a miracle, the diary survived the terrible destruction of the war years. It is in her handwriting and contains photographs. It speaks about her great love for her three children, her values, her sensitivity to the differences in us, her keen interest in our growth and development, and her desire to give to each of us whatever was best.

Until we were of school age, we had a succession of nurses who took care of us. They presided over our schedule, discipline, bathing, and meals. They were of German background and, because our parents also spoke German, the nurses taught us the language.

My older sister, Marianne, constantly rebelled against one of the nurses, who was a strict disciplinarian. I don't believe that either of us was influenced by the nurse's values, since the real world for us was that which our parents represented.

My mother was a life-giving and affirming presence in our lives. My father respected and trusted her. It was she who was primarily responsible for all the decisions affecting our lives.

As far as religious practice in the home, my parents did not follow Jewish observances. They were not members of the synagogue and never explicitly passed on any Jewish teachings. The only memory I have that relates to the Jewish faith is the Day of Atonement, a solemn fast day my mother celebrated every year with a twenty-four hour fast. I was drawn to this at an early age and joined her in the fast.

In retrospect, I realize how much wisdom of the Jewish tradition went into our upbringing. My parents' traditions, their worldview and their attitude toward life and other human beings emanated from their Jewish tradition. They never talked about it, but they instilled all these values in us.

My early experiences were recorded by my mother in the diary. It appears that, as a middle child, I tried to find my own place and role in the family. I think I may have had a hard time. My older sister was special because she was first-born, but many other things were happening when I was born. For example, my parents were remodeling our home, and then my mother became pregnant. She gave birth to my younger sister just twelve months after I was born. It seems I had to learn very early on that my parents' love needed to be shared.

Reading the diary, I learned about my first years, my relationship with my sisters, the loving way my mother observed us so closely, and how she struggled to raise us. One problem she had was that she could not breastfeed us. We had a nurse instead. I became very attached to the nurse and was very dependent on her. I searched for security in her love and care.

I was very pleased when I read in the diary that I was a very cheerful little baby and my mother and father woke up every morning to my laugh. My greatest joy, however, was when I learned that I was my father's favorite, and that the family called me "Little Elizabeth Waldmann," because I appeared to have many of my mother's characteristics.

My need for love and care must have been great in those early years. There was a time when I cried a lot for almost no reason. That was discouraged by my mother. As I grew, my mother describes me as the one easiest to handle, as an affectionate little girl who had genuine attachments.

My mother's recordings also reveal that I tried very hard in my first two years to be and do all that my older sister did and achieved. In fact, she wrote that I learned everything at an earlier age, most likely because of the stimulation and example of my sister. Later, this changed.

My older sister, Marianne, was somewhat stubborn and rebellious as a child. My younger sister, Marta was charming, original and very popular among her peers. They were both very gifted and attractive. I was shy, quiet, and I guess what you might call an introverted, feeling type. When I went to school, I always hoped to find some really good friends, but it seems that I was often disappointed. They never seemed to live up to my idea of friendship and fidelity. I was always sad because of that.

My mother left me another precious gift. She wrote it on the first page of an empty diary she gave me for my twelfth birthday. I was to record in the diary all my thoughts and feelings, which I did. But when I left Romania, I tore out this page and burned the rest of the diary.

> "I give this diary to my dear little daughter Jutka on her twelfth birthday, so that in it she will be able to express with candor the vibrations of her delicate and sensitive spirit. When you take this diary, you will not experience the loneliness that is burdensome to many people. But for you, my beloved daughter, who up until now has found in nobody that sincerity and dedication that you feel in regard to others, this diary will perhaps compensate for and will play the role of a best friend.
>
> I only wish that you will be happy and content in your life, as you deserve it. We can't help it, but God created you in this way. Keep your gentleness in the midst of the rough moments of life and engrave it deeply in your heart that you will never ever stray from the path of righteousness, so that you will be able to maintain your calm and security always in regard to every other person.
>
> Your Loving Mother, 1935."

Chapter Two

"The life of Jesus… It was like a revelation to me, and it filled my heart."

Everything my parents did was for us children. Every summer my family went away on vacation. My parents took us out of the town to a place where we could take nature hikes in the mountains, swim in the lakes and breathe fresh air. It was always such a nice time.

Before I started elementary school, my parents had a tutor teach Romanian to all of us children. We spoke Hungarian at home, but the language of the country was Romanian.

I had a very bad experience in my first year at the public school in Salonta. My teacher happened to be the principal of the school. He was a short little man, and I can still see his face. One day when he went into the city on business, he put an older boy in charge of us. I had to use the lavatory. I got permission, naturally. Three of us went, but when we returned, the principal was there. He didn't ask us anything. He just made us hold our hands out palms up. He went to his desk, took out his rod and hit us. I thought this was the end of the world. It was the first time I had ever been struck. My parents never struck us. I felt the pain and the shame. I remember it was almost time to go home, and I did not cry.

When I got home, my mother was giving a piano lesson. I did not say anything, but seeing my mother seemed to release all the pain I was holding back. Tears came to my eyes, and I quietly slipped out of the room. Seeing this, my mother realized something was wrong, and she came to my room and asked me what had happened at school.

After this incident, my parents took me out of school and got a tutor for me for a few years, until I could go into a class taught by someone other than the principal. When I did return to school, I had a woman teacher. She was such a sweet lady. I loved her and finished elementary school successfully.

In the next four years, I continued middle school and then I had to pass a difficult examination in order to be admitted into a high school.

My parents decided that I would go to the School of the Sisters of Our Lady of Sion (Sisters de Notre Dame de Sion) in Nagyvarad (Oradea). They thought it would be good for me, and they liked the idea that it was a boarding school and that many of the courses were taught in French. My older sister, Marianne, entered the school two years before I started, and I visited her often. My younger sister started at the school at the same time that I did, so we were all together.

The Sisters of Sion were mostly French and Romanian. They were brought to Nagyvarad by the Greek Catholic bishop in order to start a Catholic school, which would be available to Romanian students. There was another Catholic high school in Nagyvarad for Hungarian students, which was run by the Ursuline nuns.

The Sisters of Sion was founded in 1842 by two brothers who were Jewish converts. Alphonse and Theodore Ratisbonne were born in Strasbourg, and were sons of a well-assimilated German Jewish family.

The Sisters of Sion had a beautiful spirit. The characteristics for which they strived were charity and simplicity. They had a deep spirituality and a very open and contemporary spirit.

Their Constitution, even today, reflects this when it states, "We are called to witness by our life to God's faithful love for the Jewish people and to His fidelity to the promises He revealed to the patriarchs and prophets of Israel for all humanity. In Christ, the pledge of their fulfillment is given to us. This call implies that our apostolic life is characterized by a threefold commitment: to the Church, to the Jewish people, and to a world of justice, peace and love. Whatever task... we are engaged in, we are called to integrate in some way, these three dimensions of our apostolic commitment."

Another important reason my parents wanted us to attend this school was because it was like a safe island. Most of the other schools at that time already reflected a strong spirit of anti-Semitism, and it was difficult for those of Jewish background to be in that kind of environment.

There were Romanian, Greek Catholic and Jewish students at the boarding school. Marianne was so deeply touched by the Catholic faith she discovered when she started there in 1935, that she wanted to become Catholic right away. When she came home for vacation she would talk about it, but no one wanted to listen to her.

I was going through my own search at this time. I wanted to find my own identity as a Jewish person. I had never had a chance to experience that on a deeper level. I remember the rabbi talking about the Old Testament in my middle school religion classes, but that never touched my inner self. I was quite interested in knowing about the Jewish faith. The rabbi must have noticed this because, out of the three sisters, I was the only one invited to his house for a Seder.

During these years, there was a strong current of Zionism among the Jewish people in my town. I participated with my peers in activities sponsored by the Jewish community, such as learning Jewish songs and dances. The aim of these activities was to bring young people to an awareness of the Zionist Movement.

I was fourteen when I started at the Catholic boarding school of the Sisters of Sion. I had very good teachers, of which some were nuns and some lay teachers. However, I had a hard time being in this new environment. I thought it was a crisis to be taken away from my loving family. When I returned to school after Christmas vacation, I was very homesick. I cried all the time. I realize now that I needed to discover how to be on my own, not in the sheltered environment of my family. It was good for me to go through that, but it was very painful.

Everything was hard to get used to at the boarding school, especially the discipline. Everyone was very nice and good to me, but I was still very lonely.

What attracted me the most at school was the chapel. Most every day the Sisters gathered there for afternoon prayers. The music and the singing were beautiful, and the candles and incense made it seem like another world. I started to go to the chapel regularly.

I felt in my heart a great desire to know and understand the mystery I was experiencing. It took me a long time to overcome my shyness and finally ask my homeroom teacher, Sister Rodica, to give me something to read about the Catholic faith. She gave me a French Catechism. I began to read it and I couldn't put it down. It captivated me. The life of Jesus and everything I found in that became a revelation to me and filled my heart. This is how my faith truly started.

Prior to this, I probably searched for a God. A relationship with God was missing from my life but I didn't know it. What I do remember were good friends of my mother's who would celebrate the feast of tabernacles by putting tents up in their yards and praying. It was very mysterious to me, but I liked the ritual of it.

When I was about eleven years old, Marianne was critically ill and I remember going into our garden and crying and crying and praying to God that she would be well. I developed a prayer of petition and used it whenever there was a tragedy or whenever a crisis occurred.

I always reacted very sensitively. When the mother of a schoolmate died, I couldn't get over it. I kept wondering about the meaning of life, but

I had no answer. I was searching. I wondered, "Why were we here?" It was an existential crisis in my life.

I experienced this loneliness when I moved away from home, and I again confronted these questions about life and death. It was at this time that I discovered Jesus. A whole new world opened up for me — the meaning of life, the purpose of existence, living, loving, and dying. Everything just made sense. All of a sudden, I had the answers to every question, even the questions I was unable to articulate before.

I slowly became a Christian without even knowing it. I rejoiced in the new vision I acquired – a vision that filled my heart and my mind. I went to church, and I didn't think I needed to do any formal thing. I just thought I needed to live my life as a Christian.

I had a wonderful role model in Sister Rodica. She was a beautiful Christian, who taught French literature, psychology and philosophy. She was extremely bright and profound, a very intense and authentic person. Everything she taught was permeated with the Christian vision.

During the summer, when my sisters and I were home on vacation, we spent a few weeks in a beautiful resort in Transylvania. We met up with old friends, and every day I went to a little church that was located there. My Jewish friends saw me going to church and they asked what was happening to me. They began to tell me all about their Jewish faith and ask me questions about the Christian faith. I couldn't answer them, because I didn't know enough. I was feeling confused and suffered so much in my heart because I didn't know what to believe anymore. There were so many questions. What had seemed clear before I now began to doubt. I suffered intensely.

Then I came home and visited Sister Rodica. She gave me a wonderful prayer and that stayed with me: "O God, grant me the light of your truth. Grant me the love of your will. And give me the courage to be faithful to you. May YOU be my light, my strength and my love."

That's what I prayed, and I prayed intensely that God would show me where the truth and light were, and that I would have the courage to follow them. This is how I spent my days and my nights – praying.

Toward the end of that summer, my cousin George came to visit us. He was the son of my uncle who had become Catholic. George was ten years older than I, and he had been raised a Catholic and was deeply religious. Two years prior to our summer meeting, he had decided to become a Trappist monk. The whole family tried to convince him not to become a monk, including me. We all thought it was terrible, because we could not understand the meaning or motivation behind such a choice.

He came to visit us that summer to say good-bye. His father had arranged for him to leave Hungary and go to Australia because the danger to the Jewish people in Europe was growing.

George was such a believer. That summer, which was the last time I ever saw him, he spent ten days with us. I shared with him that I was going through a faith crisis and wanted to become Catholic. We spent days and nights together talking about God. He answered all my questions and addressed all my doubts, because he was so profoundly living his faith. I felt I got a course in apologetics, he was so knowledgeable. He seemed to know everything.

Gradually, my peace came back and the light came back, and the truth came together again. All the questions I had just disappeared, and I was strengthened once more in my newfound faith.

While all this was going on in my heart, Hitler was in full sway in the world. The Jews were persecuted in Germany and other parts of Europe. The ominous spread of anti-Semitism was prevalent. My parents, fully aware of these realities, were very fearful, just like all the other Jewish people. They began to plan for us to flee Romania.

My father's brother, Emeric, who lived in Budapest, was a businessman. While traveling on business, he discovered that Australia was a safe place, ready to receive Jewish immigrants. He moved there with his family and established himself.

Emeric sent us all the papers and the affidavit to join him there and we were ready to go. It was my father's hope to sell everything – the house and the pharmacy – in order to get enough money for travel expenses for the whole family, as well as to get established once we were there.

The pharmacy was sold, and the new co-owner came to live in Salonta. All we were waiting for was the approval of the state. The pharmacy was under the control of the state, so we needed approval to sell it. The government rejected the request and would not allow my father to sell his property. This was one way the government stopped Jewish people from leaving.

For us, everything was frustrating. For my father, it was particularly devastating and frightening not to get us out of Romania. My father continued to help many other people. People found out that he had a brother in Australia, so they came to him. He arranged for many people from Oradea and other cities all over Transylvania to go to Australia.

His pharmacy and office became a meeting place for these people, and my father mediated all the arrangements with my uncle. He was very happy to do this. We, however, never left. My father and mother agonized over our being trapped in Romania. They recognized that we children were already oriented toward Catholicism, and decided that perhaps we should, as a family, become Catholic. They thought it might mean our survival. Many Jews were becoming Christians, trying to escape persecution.

In the fall of 1938, when we returned to school, the decision was made that the family would formally become Catholic. This decision was not that important to me at the time because the vision in my heart was sufficient for me. I already had found peace and truth.

According to the laws of the country, female children could not change their faith unless their mother changed her faith. My mother was ready to embrace the Christian faith. My father, however, although he never practiced his Jewish faith, felt he could not leave that tradition.

My mother went to the pastor in Salonta for catechism. My sisters and I received the religious training we needed at the school of the Sisters of Sion. It was a special grace of God that the pastor in Salonta at that time was such an open-minded person. His name was Father Banass, and he was the future bishop of Veszprem.

My mother was very receptive. She received everything very openly in great faith. Through her catechism lessons, she embraced the faith wholeheartedly. She became a practicing Catholic, something we children never dreamed would happen.

On my mother's feast day, November 19, 1938, my mother, sisters, and I were baptized. On the following day, in the same chapel of the Sisters of Sion, we had our first communion.

Reflecting back on this time, it seemed I was a little fearful of the formal commitment of baptism. I wondered if I would live up to it. I don't think I would have sought baptism because believing in Jesus fully satisfied me. At the same time, I understood, on some level, that baptism would allow me to more fully participate in the life of Jesus. My first communion was something I experienced as a tremendous mystery, and I became a daily communicant. I couldn't miss one day, so every morning I went to six o'clock Mass in the chapel.

As time went on, my father realized that he couldn't live with the idea that religion would separate the family. After a great deal of agonizing, he decided to seek baptism. He wanted to be one with us. One year later, he was baptized. He never practiced the Catholic religion, but he did what he felt was right in his heart.

I must admit, that at this point in my development, I was unable to grasp the terrible reality of the persecution of the Jewish people. My parents were able to see it, but I wasn't. I was even less able to imagine the course it would take. For me at that time, being a Christian meant living in Jesus, experiencing His wisdom and His power, and following His path. The way I learned Christianity was not as a rejection of the Jewish tradition, but as a completion of it. The New Testament was the fulfillment of the Old Testament.

In retrospect, I can say that the Catholic faith enabled me to experience my connectedness to the absolute, incomprehensible God. It enabled me to find in God all I most desired: infinite love, meaning and ultimately, peace.

Chapter Three

"I give thanks to the risen Lord for my life, and I share my story to praise God's name. This was my call to religious life."

I chose Lilla Wittman to be my godmother. She was just two years older than I, and attended the school of the Sisters of Sion with me. She was a senior and was preparing to become a Sister. (Today she is known as Sister Judith of the Sisters of Sion.) We were distant relatives, but we didn't know it at the time. Her father was Christian, but her mother was of Jewish background. Like me, she also was a convert. I had great respect for her, and we were good friends.

During our Christmas vacation in 1938, she came to my parents' house in Salonta to spend a few days with us. We shared some beautiful talks about God. At some point she said to me, "Judith, I think you have a call to the religious life."

That struck me very deeply. I wondered how she could say something like that. It disturbed me very much. Up to that moment, I always considered a "normal" life for myself: a life of marriage, children and family. How could I ever think of anything else? In a way, I thought that religious life was the most sublime life, so how could I ever be called to it? It seemed unbelievable to me. On the other hand, I also saw all the implications and I wondered how I could ever follow that call. I knew my parents would never consent to it. But from that moment on, the search for my vocation began in my heart. I prayed, struggled and tried to discover what was right. I cried out to God and asked, "Show me! Is this really a call? Are You calling me?"

There was no answer for a long time. I suffered in the depths of my heart. I wanted to respond to God's call but did not know what His will was for me.

I read the book, *Hear the Call*, and deeply identified with it. It is about the life of the prophet Jeremiah and his struggle with being called. I was deeply affected by the book because I felt I was going through the same struggle, asking God, "Why me? Why this calling? Is it possible?"

About a year and a half later, in 1940, during Holy Week, God somehow responded to my prayers. I was in my junior year of high school, and the Sisters of Sion invited me to spend Holy Week with them. Prior to that week, I never was exposed to that kind of atmosphere. I spent the whole time in prayer. There wasn't any community retreat; I just spent the time participating in the mystery of the agony and death of Christ.

It was the experience of Jesus' passion that touched my heart so deeply. I experienced the incomprehensible love of Jesus for all of us, the human race, and for me, personally, in a very profound way. It was through this experience that I felt in my own heart the power to accept the invitation and to respond to it. I was empowered. I received the grace to surrender my life completely to God. I knew that it was, humanly speaking, impossible to foresee how I would be able to respond to my call, but I felt that I received the grace and the gift to respond with my whole life to that invitation. It was a very important moment in my life — an experience of grace, of being touched by God, and being assured, in some way, that I would be able to follow the call. It was a deep inner experience.

I envisioned my life of consecration to God as a Sister of Sion because that was where I had come to know Christ. It seemed natural to me. Of course, I could not talk about this with my family; I knew they would not understand.

God sent me a spiritual director, Father Ioan Suciu, a very holy man, who returned to Romania after studying in Rome. I met him when he gave a retreat to the students at the School of the Sisters of Sion. He was a Greek Catholic priest who was soon named Bishop of Oradea. Later in his life, he was imprisoned by the Communists and died a martyr's death in prison.

Shortly after he came to Nagyvarad to live, he accepted my request for him to be my spiritual director. It was with him that I shared my longing and my questioning about how I could follow my call, and how I could help my parents understand this call. I went to see him quite often. He gave me beautiful meditations and helped me get more deeply into the spiritual life. In his great wisdom and compassion, he encouraged me to wait for the moment when I could follow my vocation without causing pain to my parents.

He told me, "Judith, you have to wait. God will show you. You will know when the moment is there to really follow your vocation. Just believe in it. Believe that God will indicate it to you in some way. The doors will open and you will be able to follow your call. Just wait." He gave me courage, and he helped me to wait.

Other things happened during those years. In 1940, part of Transylvania was annexed to Hungary. The Sisters of Sion could not continue in Nagyvarad because the school did not have any teachers who spoke Hungarian. They closed the school in 1941, and the Sisters went to other places, like Romania and France. When they left, I experienced a great loss, since they were such a source of support for me. In my desire to maintain a relationship with the congregation, I contacted the Sisters of Sion in Budapest. I wrote to them, visited them, and again found the support I needed.

In 1941, I graduated from high school and applied for admission to medical school. My parents had a dream that I would be a doctor. However, because of "numerus clausus," restrictive laws that only allowed a small percentage of Jewish students to be accepted into the universities, I was rejected.

It was on the day of my high school graduation that I learned of the School of Social Work in Kolozsvar, Hungary from Clara Scholtz, an associate member of the Sisters of Social Service. I was so happy when I heard about it. I felt that by attending that school, I would learn what it means to help people and how to go about it. The idea of attending the School of Social Work appealed so much to me that I told my parents I wanted to go there. My parents would have preferred that I receive some training in a practical field, like a seamstress, so I could support myself, since laws excluded Jews from professional fields, but they finally agreed.

I sent in my application and Sister Lidia, the very personable and caring director, graciously responded that she would accept me. In the fall of 1941, I arrived in Kolozsvar. It was my first contact with the Sisters of Social Service, and I was extremely pleased with all I experienced. The faculty, the program and the environment were stimulating, enriching and meaningful. I felt the experience would enable me to live out more fully the gospel call of being for others, alleviate human suffering, share God's love with the poor, and give hope to those in darkness. The spirit of the school was very freeing, human, inclusive, and contemporary.

In the spring of 1942, my father died of heart disease at the age of fifty-two. The Jewish laws of Hungary made life increasingly difficult for him. My father tried again to sell the pharmacy, and the second time around it seemed it would be possible, but all the struggles and hardships took their toll on his health. I believe he died of a broken heart. All that he hoped for seemed to have been unattainable. His family ended up trapped.

He suffered for two years before he died. My mother and all of us

16

were in deep grief, but I was comforted by God. I knew my father would find eternal joy because God's love is stronger and greater than ours. I believed that God loved my father, and I knew my father was a man of God, a man for others and a father who cared. He was a man of goodness and compassion. Deep in my heart I knew he was in God's love, and this sustained me in this time of great loss.

In the months following my father's death, I felt a sense of urgency in following my call. I again contacted the Sisters of Sion and formally expressed my desire to be accepted into their community. I told no one about this, but it was at this time that my mother found out about my vocation. I spent my summer vacation in Salonta. When I returned to Kolozsvar, a response to my request came from the Sisters of Sion to my mother's home. It said I was welcome to join them. My mother read the letter and found out about my wanting to be accepted into the community. She was totally devastated at the thought. She couldn't imagine that I could find happiness in any other way than she had. She wrote me a letter and then she came to visit me. She told me that she could never agree to my becoming a Sister. She said, "Everything in me is against it. It is not for you. I want you to be happy as I have been happy. Each cell in me resists this."

While all this was happening, I was living in Kolozsvar and studying at the School of Social Work, which was one of the special programs offered by the Sisters of Social Service. The founding Sisters had not wanted to be a teaching order, because there were so many of those already in the country. Instead, they wanted to serve marginalized people. Therefore, they decided the only kind of educational institution they would have would be one that promoted social consciousness. Their aim was to sensitize young people to the needs of the victimized segments of society – especially women, children and families – and address the root causes of the social problems affecting the lives of these victimized groups.

With the annexation of Transylvania to Hungary in 1940, there was an urgent need to train workers for the public welfare system. The program I attended at the School of Social Work was a response to this need. It lasted twelve months and included both theoretical and field practice components. My class was one of the first to graduate.

In the fall of 1942, there was a retreat for all of us who graduated from the School of Social Work. A Jesuit priest, Father Kardos, came to Kolozsvar and gave the beautiful retreat. I went to him and told him that I wanted to give my life to God, but I could not join a community. I explained my mother's feelings about religious life and her resistance to my choice. It was at that point he advised me to take a private vow. I took a private vow of celibacy for one year.

Shortly after the retreat, I started my career as a social worker. Because of my Jewish background, it was not possible for me to be employed in the public welfare system where most of the graduates went to work. I was, however, hired by the Diocesan Office for Diaspora Service. The Diocese had a special program that gave pastoral care to all Catholic people living in the Diaspora. This included people scattered all over and living in small groups – maybe one or two families, maybe ten families – people who for years and years had not seen a priest. Many of these people lived in the mountains.

It was a fascinating job. My boss was Father Laszlo David, who eventually died in Kolozsvar in the 1990s. We worked together very closely. My job was to discover the isolated groups, visit them, and then find out about their spiritual and material needs. I was nineteen years old when I started, and many times I traveled by bicycle. I would arrive at a railway station and there would be no other transportation from there. This meant I would use the bicycle I brought with me on the train. I had a whole route. Sometimes on my second visit, people would come to meet and welcome me. It was a beautiful ministry because I had so much personal contact with the people, and because these people had a great hunger and thirst for a deeper life in God.

While I worked for the diocese and made these site visits, I lived in a building that was located on the grounds of the Provincial House of the Sisters of Social Service. The Sisters lived in the Provincial Center, which also was the building that housed the School of Social Work. The building I lived in was for graduates of the school who already were working. It was like a family house. It had two floors, about ten rooms and a common kitchen. Several of us lived there at that time, and we were physically very close to the Sisters, so I maintained a friendly relationship with them. I loved the Sisters, respected them, and appreciated their openness to me, but I never for a moment thought I would become a Sister of Social Service; I always thought I was called to be a Sister of Sion.

It was during this time that my vocation was tested. I fell in love. He was a university student, a good Christian, and very religious. We didn't date, but I felt something deep inside of me. I got to know him because he sometimes came to the office where I worked. My boss was his spiritual director and also was his teacher. It was very hard because I had a great liking for him, and I could imagine something more developing between us. I struggled with this, and I started to doubt my call. It was a year of inner struggle because my vow was being tested.

Toward the end of that year, in the fall of 1943, I attended a second retreat. I was trying to decide whether or not I should renew my private vow for another year. I was advised to live without the vow and just let God reveal to me what my call was to be.

Chapter Four

"It was in the year of 1944 that God's call was manifested to me in a dramatic way."

Between the years of 1940-1944, there were many things happening in Hungary that indicated the country was moving in the direction of Nazism. There were regulations that restricted the rights and equal citizenship of the Jewish people, and most able-bodied Jewish men forcibly were taken to labor camps.

In the spring of 1944, when the Nazi Army entered Hungary, the persecution of the Jewish people reached its climax. In March 1944, every person of Jewish background was ordered to wear a yellow star so he/she could be easily identified.

People who were well informed knew what was going on in other countries occupied by the Nazis. Millions of people already had been deported from Poland, Austria and other European countries. The hearts of the Jewish people of Hungary were filled with anguish because of these ominous measures. And what was feared did materialize. Ghettoes were set up in most of the cities of Hungary. By May 1944, the deportations began.

These oppressive policies affected my life. As Father David explained to me at the time, the yellow star was only the beginning. It was used to identify Jews, who subsequently were taken to the ghettoes and then deported.

I could no longer walk the street safely, do my traveling work or work at the office where I assisted. Father David wanted me to continue my work, but he did not want me on the road or out of my house. He told me he would bring my work to me and I could continue it at home. He told me not to leave home because someone might know of my background, see I was not wearing the star and notify the authorities. For the next five weeks, I worked in seclusion in my room in the building that housed lay social workers.

I remember how much it meant to me that a dear friend, Elizabeth Keresztes, who graduated with me from the School of Social Work, came to visit me with her husband, Alexander. They were so supportive and loving to me during those difficult times.

The critical moment soon arrived — all the Jewish people who lived in Kolozsvar were to be taken to the ghetto by May 5, 1944. I decided I did not want to go to the ghetto in Kolozsvar; I wanted to join my mother and sisters in Salonta where a ghetto had not yet been set up. I felt, rather than be alone in the Kolozsvar ghetto, I wanted to be with my family for whatever was going to happen to us.

When Father David learned what I was going to do, he became deeply concerned, and felt he must prevent it at all costs. He agonized over the situation and said to me, "You don't know what all this means and where all this will lead. I want you to be saved. You don't know the terrible things that will happen." He showed vast concern for me. He was a man with a great heart who did not know what to do to save me. He went to the Sisters of Social Service and asked Sister Augusta if she would shelter me, so my life could be spared. Sister Augusta knew this could have very serious consequences because the penalty for hiding a Jewish person was very harsh. She knew the whole community could be punished if they sheltered me.

The Sisters also were aware that the law at that time exempted Sisters from the restrictions. For that reason, they decided to take the risk and consider me already a member. They took this upon themselves, even though up to that point, I was not a member of the community.

Sister Augusta, in her great wisdom and love, said to me, "Judith, we are doing this because we love you and we want you to live. We would be the happiest people in the world if, when this is over, we could give you back to your mother or the Sisters of Sion."

They wanted to give me absolute freedom. They wanted me to know that just because they were doing this, I did not have any obligation to join their community.

I was so torn in my heart between joining my mother and sisters or finally accepting this invitation to follow my call. I agonized over it. Father David went to visit my mother. My two sisters were with her in Salonta.

My older sister, Marianne, was married and nearly at the end of her first pregnancy. Her husband already had been taken away to a labor camp. My younger sister, Marta, had finished high school, but like most Jewish people, she could not get a decent job. When the Hungarian Army entered Salonta in 1940, one of the young officers fell in love with her. This Hungarian officer's family lived in Budapest, so my sister went there after her high school graduation in 1942 to live with our relatives and to be close to him. His family owned a business and could give her a job. When the bombing of Budapest began, my mother was concerned that Marta would be killed, so she asked her to come home and be with her in a safer place.

When Father David saw my mother, he told her he would like to be my guardian, and that he had asked the Sisters of Social Service to shelter and hide me as a member of their community. He asked her if she would consent to this. He also explained that I would not be obligated in any way to really join the Sisters' community. The offer was just a gesture of love and concern. He said, "Her freedom to choose her own life and to return to you will always be hers."

My mother, deeply aware of the critical situation that she, her family, and all Jewish people found themselves in, wholeheartedly welcomed the offer of life for one of her daughters. She wished there was a salvation for all. The survival of her children was more important than anything else, and at that point it was her only concern. The fact that one of her daughters could be saved was the only consolation she could find in the midst of her present distress. The one request my mother had, if she were to survive what was to come, was that I spend a year with her, so I would have another chance to freely decide about my future.

Father David returned to Kolozsvar and told me my mother's response. For the many years I waited to follow my call, I could never have imagined the time would come when I could give my life to God in a way that would not be painful to my mother, but would instead, in some way, bring her consolation. That seemed inconceivable to me.

Reflecting on my mother's response, I now was faced with the most difficult decision I ever had to make. The question in my heart was, "What is the greater love, to be where my mother and sisters are and to share a common destiny, or to follow my call and give my life to God?" What gave me the courage to decide was my mother's love. Her love indicated that she really wanted me to accept the offer of life. I recognized God's will for me. It was the beginning of a sacred journey to which I was called, and it was a moment of fulfillment and inexplicable awe at the Mystery of God. God opened the door for me, so that I could finally give my life irrevocably to Him.

I remember that first night. I kept thinking, "Is this really happening?" The longing of all those years finally was fulfilled. The obstacles vanished. I felt, in a sense, that I was truly God's and God was mine. I could hardly believe it. At the same time that I was experiencing this mystery, I also was feeling a terrible pain for my mother and sisters and all Jewish people. But in the depth of my being, I heard Christ speak these words to me, "The greatest love one can have for one's friends is to give one's life for them." In that moment, I knew my surrender to God and my whole life was intimately bound with another call, that of the giving of my life for my beloved ones.

I accepted the offer of the Sisters of Social Service. For my protection, Sister Augusta made out an official certificate that stated, "Judith Fenyvesi took her vows in 1942. She is a member of our community." This date was decided on because it was the date of my private vows. I also was given the grey uniform that the Sisters of Social Service wore at that time. My novitiate was to coincide with the last year of World War II and the two years following that.

The Sisters of Social Service sent me to the novitiate in Nagyvarad because they thought someone might get suspicious if they saw me in Kolozsvar. I suddenly appeared at the novitiate in my grey uniform, and all the novices wondered who I was. It was very puzzling for them because only third year novices wore the grey uniform, and they didn't know there was another third year novice.

I arrived in Nagyvarad on May 1, 1944. Between that date and June 27, many painful things happened. It was during that time I was able to visit my mother and sisters. They had not moved into a ghetto, because since there were so few Jewish people in Salonta, a ghetto was not set up there. They were, by law, confined to their homes, and they had permission to leave only between nine and ten in the morning.

We met in the rectory of the Catholic Church. The priest was brave enough to allow us to meet there. I could travel freely because I was wearing the uniform of a religious, and religious were exempt from the restrictions. Another Sister of Social Service accompanied me.

It was a most painful hour that we spent together. We talked about the possibility of their escape and of the Sisters of Social Service giving them shelter. My family, however, was unable to take the risk, mainly because so many others tried and were killed. It seemed too dangerous. They thought it would be worse if they tried and were caught. It was already too late, but we talked about it anyway. They had a dim hope that the deportations would never happen, especially since Salonta did not even have a ghetto.

After my visit with my family, I was haunted by the thought of how I could save my mother and sisters. Now that I was saved, how could I be instrumental in saving them? I tried to think of a way to get them out, so they, too, could live. It was a time of personal agony.

It also was at this time that Sister Margaret Slachta, the Foundress of the Sisters of Social Service, came to Nagyvarad to speak at a Pentecost retreat for the Sisters. All she talked about at the retreat was, if we are Christians, we must recognize Jesus in all persons, and even more so in persecuted people.

Sister Margaret shared with the Sisters her understanding of God's call. Her heart was filled with deep concern for what was happening to the Jewish people. She knew she had to speak out against this horrendous evil. She tried to be the "voice crying out in the desert." Now, she fearlessly and untiringly worked to help the helpless people and to stop the inhumanities. She left no stone unturned.

Inspired by Sister Margaret and attentive to her prophetic voice, the Sisters knew that no compromise was possible. They, too, committed themselves to respond to God's call and were willing to pay the price — to lay down their lives for the persecuted ones.

While in the center of the city Jews were being gathered into the ghetto, loaded onto cattle wagons, and sent to strange lands and an unknown fate, Sister Margaret, in the silence of the retreat, asked the question, "Are we willing, in the name of Christian love, to take the risk of being interred or carried away, or of the community being dissolved or even of losing our own lives?" In the following months, in the many homes of the Sisters all over the country, persecuted people found shelter. There were continuously more than a thousand people housed by the Sisters.

It was during this retreat that I decided to open my heart and soul to Sister Margaret. I asked her what I could do to save my mother and sisters. We started talking about how I could bring them to the Sisters so they would be safe. While we were making these plans, I was called to the parlor, and I learned that on the previous day, all the Jewish people of Salonta had been brought to the ghetto of Nagyvarad. It was my birthday, June 8th. At that moment, all seemed irreversible. The illusion that the Jewish people of Salonta would not be deported was shattered.

I was still able to visit my mother twice in the ghetto because I was protected by being considered a member of the Sisters of Social Service. I do not recall exactly the date when, in my pain, I went back to Ioan Suciu, the Greek Catholic Bishop. He received me with great compassion. He said, "Why did you not contact me sooner? There is someone here in the city who is involved in smuggling people out of the ghetto." He offered to connect me with him. I do not recall whether I actually met the person, but I learned for that service, the person expected to be paid.

I spent my days trying to get the money and working on the escape plan for my loved ones. I was told this plan would work and I believed it. On June 26, 1944, I was making every possible effort to insure that an escape would happen. I did not return to the convent for the whole day. When I did return, a message was waiting for me.

The commander of the ghetto had been put up in the home of a friend, Delia Polgar. Through her relationship with this commander, she was able to get my mother out of the ghetto under the pretext that my mother was going to clean the commander's living quarters. The real goal was for my mother and me to have a final visit together. I learned in the message I received that evening that my mother waited the whole day, hoping I could be reached, so she could say good-bye to me.

I cannot describe the pain I felt. It is beyond words. I missed this last chance. On June 27, the deportations began. My loved ones did not escape. They were not smuggled out. In spite of all my efforts to stop it, my mother, grandmother, and two sisters were deported. I learned, forty-eight years later, in a letter from Father David, that they were on a garbage cart being smuggled out of the ghetto when the ghetto commander stopped them and ordered them off the cart.

I lived through this horror only by the great love I experienced and the great faith God put in my heart. My surrender to God and my awareness of my call gained new breadth and depth. Intrinsic to my call now was a burning desire that God would accept me, and in some mysterious way, all that I was, and all I would be, would somehow serve the creation of a world based on love, humanity and justice.

What filled my heart was a deep identification with the suffering of Christ, and the suffering of all people, including my loved ones and all Jewish people. What sustained me and gave me strength was a deep belief that all this suffering, including my own pain, would not be lost but would have meaning.

Chapter Five

"We praise God with you for the great marvels that God has done for you..."

After the deportation of my mother, grandmother, and sisters, my life was to continue on a difficult path. Knowing the trauma I suffered, Sister Augusta planned a time of quiet and rest for me. She sent me to the mountain resort area of Marosfo where the Sisters had a simple little cottage. It was a very tranquil place in the middle of a forest.

After two or three weeks in Marosfo, I returned to Nagyvarad and joined the other novices of Transylvania. We then left for Szegvar where we joined all the first year novices of the Hungarian District.

This was at the end of July. By August 24, 1944, Romania surrendered and joined forces with the invading Russians. An estimated 200,000 Hungarians in Northern Transylvania were killed, imprisoned, tortured, and/or deported to labor camps.

The Russian Army advanced further west by September. The Germans began to withdraw, and we found ourselves caught in a war zone. Szegvar was in danger of being invaded by the Russians. It was a frightening experience, because wherever the Russian Army went, they raped every woman they could find.

Fearing for the novices, the novitiate was evacuated. The leadership of the Sisters of Social Service tried to figure out how to help the novices survive without sending them to their homes. Other communities had sent their novices home to rather uncertain fates.

Our leaders tried to do everything to protect us. They put us into separate smaller groups, so if one group fell into danger, the other would survive. No one was safe, especially in Budapest, where constant bombing attacks took place.

When Szegvar was evacuated, we went to Budapest to catch a train for our first destination, Denesfa. We bought a group ticket and tried to board the train. It was so crowded with others trying to escape that it was almost impossible to get on. People were sitting on the steps and were crowded into the aisles. A few of us had to throw our suitcases through an open window, and then ask a soldier standing on the platform to lift us up and push us through the window onto the train.

We could not find the other novices on the train. When we were asked for our tickets, we realized some of our group had not boarded, including the novice director with the tickets. We were allowed to stay on until we reached the city of Gyor, where it was confirmed that our novice mistress and five novices were not with us.

We continued on until we reached Szombathely. At this station, an air raid siren went off and we had to go into a shelter. It was after this I learned my suitcase with everything I owned in it was stolen from the luggage carrier above my seat on the train.

We went into the city to look for the home of a Sister of Social Service who lived there. We stayed only until that afternoon, when we boarded the train again for Denesfa. When we arrived there, we went to an empty school. It was a very primitive place with no beds and no food. We were fortunate to get some food from the townspeople. We stayed there for about three weeks. Then we were forced by the German Army to abandon this place because they claimed the school to house their soldiers. We felt lost, and had nowhere to go.

We heard that another group of novices was staying on the shore of Lake Balaton. Again we boarded a train, risking our very lives due to the constant airplane attacks. We reached a place called Jankovicstelep on October 15. Sister Elizabeth Bokor, a founding member of the Sisters of Social Service, invited us to join her at Zamardi, where a summer camp for the poor children of Budapest was located. The camp was empty because the season was over. However, we only stayed there for two weeks because of the danger. The Russians were still moving toward us.

There were other places and more hardships on this journey of escape, but we finally got an offer from Father George Kis, pastor in a small village called Romand. The other members of our novice group, who had been missing on the train, made their way to Romand before us, and we joined them. We were received into the rectory of Father Kis, where all fourteen of us novices and our two novice directors lived. We began our regular novitiate program there. We studied, took care of the sacristy and did some housework.

When the village people of Romand were forced by the Nazis to dig trenches around the village, we had to dig, too. It was a cold and hard winter, living in constant terror of the Russians and what they would do to us. It was thought that if we looked like nuns the Russians would not rape us. As such, we put on long black dresses and started to wear veils, even though these habits were not part of the Sisters of Social Service's tradition.

We hoped these costumes would protect us.

In the following months, Budapest was under siege and there was no communication to or from the capital. We were cut off from all the other Sisters and all other parts of the country, some of which already were occupied by the Russians. We did not know when the Russians would reach us, but we knew that day would come.

The Russians reached us in March 1945. The Nazis fled when the Russians started firing mortar shells on the town. We fled with the villagers into the hills until the shelling stopped. When we returned to the village, we went through terrible days and nights of fear. The Russians went from house to house looking for Nazi soldiers, raping women, and taking what they wanted. They came to the rectory, too. No one could communicate with them because no one spoke Russian. We told them we were religious women, using the Russian word for "religious," but it meant nothing to them.

One of the Russian soldiers forced me into an empty room and tried to attack me. I don't remember how, but I saw an open window. I jumped out of it and ran. He chased me with his gun drawn. I just kept running and running. I ran down a path that led to an adjoining village. My fear grew even more when I realized the path was full of more Russian soldiers. It can only be a miracle that they let me pass.

When I reached the other village, I hid in a root cellar where other farm workers were hiding. The Russians also were hunting down these people. No one knew when they would pound on the door and take someone away. Father Kis, who had been away from the rectory when the Russians arrived, finally tracked me down to the root cellar and came to save me. All of the Sisters were then split up and put into different hiding places.

On May 7, 1945, the war ended. Northern Transylvania was returned to Romania, and the borders were closed between Romania and Hungary. Sister Augusta wanted the Transylvanian novices to return. The Hungarian novices stayed in Romand for a few more months.

On our way to Transylvania, our group of four first went to Budapest. The four of us traveled, and slept in train cattle cars with other refugees who had fled Transylvania, and who were now going home. Under normal conditions, this trip takes four or five hours, but it took us two weeks. We lived under miserable conditions with no food or water. The train would stop, and we would sit on the grass for days until it would start again.

After we finally reached Romania, I stopped in Nagyvarad to ask about my family. I also went to Salonta to see if I could find out anything. I was still hoping that some of my family would return. There were stories of some people surviving. Some, I was told, were just too weak to travel. In Salonta, I tried to discover what might have happened to my family. I hadn't given up hope. I thought that maybe at a later time they would still come home.

But, I never heard anything about my family after they were deported. My grandmother, who was eighty years old, was deported with my mother and two sisters. From what I know now, all the older, sick and pregnant women immediately were sent to the gas chambers. Some of the pregnant women were taken to those terrible places where they did experiments. All I know is that my older sister and grandmother were never seen again with my mother and younger sister.

Two women, who also were deported, returned to Salonta after the war. One was the wife of a doctor, Mrs. Grunbaum. The other, Mrs. Preis, was the mother of one of my schoolmates. My schoolmate never came back, nor did her father. Mrs. Preis was the only survivor. Both of these women told me they were taken from Auschwitz with my mother and younger sister to another camp where they had to work. Everything was so vague to them. They couldn't remember timeframes, or when they last had seen my mother and sister. But they did remember that one day, when an SS Soldier came and asked if anyone wanted to be excused from work, my mother and sister presented themselves.

Everyone knew that if you answered, you would be sent to the gas chambers. Mrs. Grunbaum and Mrs. Preis both said that my mother, even though she knew what would happen, may have felt she just couldn't go on. Perhaps she and my sister were so weak that they just gave up. The conditions my mother and sister lived in were atrocious.

That's all I found out. I didn't learn what camp it was; I only knew that they worked for a while. During the war, I received one card from them. It contained just two lines. After the war, I heard that the Nazis gave prisoners permission to write a card and send it home, so people would believe they were okay. That card gave me hope for a long time, but they never came back. It was not until fifty years later that I was to know their fate.

After I and the other three novices finally reached Cluj, Romania and resumed our regular novitiate program, I saw Sister Augusta again. I officially requested membership in the community of the Sisters of Social Service. However, before speaking to her, I wrote to the Sisters of Sion because I had previously committed myself to joining them. I told them how the Sisters of Social Service saved my life. I was still trying to search out where God was calling me.

The Sisters of Sion responded to me beautifully. "We praise God with you for the great marvels that God has done for you, and we encourage you and affirm you to be a member of that community which so generously accepted and saved you."

In Cluj, food was scarce and conditions were hard following the war. But I persevered, and I completed the School of Social Work prior to entering the community. Sisters who were not trained to be social workers were encouraged to take the social work courses.

There also were training programs for catechists that prepared them for church ministry. I took this program, which consisted of one year of classes and one year of practical experience. I majored in religious education with courses in catechism, theology, church history, and dogmatics.

By the following spring, I was sick with colitis. Apparently, all the inner suffering got to me. I had terrible attacks. I could not eat anything without getting sick. Even though food was scarce, the Sisters did everything to try and get food that I could eat. I had a very obstinate type of colitis and was in poor condition physically.

Sister Augusta looked after me. She asked me to work with her, sorting out her correspondence and filing. She was extremely affirming, treating me with great affection. It was during those times that we would talk together. She was always able to convey total acceptance.

I got very weak from the colitis, and I lost weight. Ultimately, I came down with pleurisy and tuberculosis. I had a high temperature for four to six weeks. I kept returning to the doctor, who would remove fluid from my lungs. Everyone was concerned about what would happen to me. I was instructed to rest for a number of hours every day and not to do any physical work. My blood was constantly checked to see if the TB was still there. I missed a few weeks of school, but I managed to complete my training program, which proved to be helpful since my first ministry was teaching catechism.

In February 1947, four of us were sent to Budapest to prepare ourselves for our first profession. Sister Augusta had a deep conviction that we should experience our one-ness with all the Sisters and with all the community. She knew certain things were possible in Hungary that were not possible in Romania, and that we also would meet our Foundress, Sister Margaret.

It was a dangerous trip, but Sister Augusta arranged everything. We crossed the border illegally because there was no communication between Romania and Hungary. People were not supposed to cross because conditions in both countries were so unsettled. The borders were closed, but we went anyway, each of us carrying a little bag.

We went to a city in northwest Romania where people took a chance and crossed the border. Our Sisters had found out about it and knew where to go. We crossed a big field in the dark of night in the snow. It was a very dangerous adventure, but we finally got to Hungary, and then we took a train to Budapest. We were received with great love and were integrated into the routine of the novitiate.

It was an excellent experience. We were there for the three months before our profession. Sister Augusta, however, was concerned about my health. Usually, Sisters accepted for profession had to be healthy. Sister Augusta asked the Provincial in Budapest, Sister Paula Ronai, to do everything she could so I would get better. They sent me to a specialist and a miraculous thing happened. The doctor they found had worked on a vaccine for TB, which he gave to me. I received the vaccine twice, and I was healed, although I remained under observation and needed to return several times.

During this time, I had the privilege of participating in some of the classes Sister Margaret taught in the School of Social Work. She talked to us about the importance of lobbying and her political ministry. She believed we were called to act as lobbyists, and she explained how important it was to express our convictions to the politicians. This was her pioneering ministry. On several occasions, I went to the Parliament to hear Sister Margaret speak.

I also remember the meditations Sister Paula gave the novices. They were very life-giving. A month before Pentecost, we went to a place near Budapest called Remetekertvaros. It was a marvelous time for prayer, reflection, and preparing ourselves for our first vows. Sisters preparing themselves for their final vows were there, also.

We stayed at a lovely house with beautiful grounds, good air and peaceful mornings. It was almost like a villa. A Benedictine father preached a retreat for us in this rustic spiritual atmosphere. It was a very contemplative time.

On May 25, 1947, in the early morning, the novices and I took the streetcar to the Motherhouse for our first profession and a big celebration.

While in Budapest, I also visited my mother's brother and his family before I went back to Romania. The other novices went back before me. I crossed the border again, and although I was not with the Sisters, I had another woman companion with me. We were lucky not to be caught. Many who were caught were put in jail.

Very soon after this, I got my first assignment and was sent to Bucharest, Romania to do catechetical work and youth ministry. I was sent there because I spoke Romanian very well. There were just a few Sisters in Bucharest at that time. The original home of the Sisters was bombed during the war, so we lived in a little apartment. There were just four rooms and one of the rooms was a chapel. Three of us lived in that little apartment, and two other sisters lived in a room in the rectory of the Hungarian Church.

I was immediately assigned to the Cathedral Parish and I started the catechetical work. The university students were a part of my work, and my pastor was Monsignor Joseph Shubert. There were not many Catholics in Bucharest; the majority of Romanians were Greek Orthodox. I prepared children and teenagers for first communion and confirmation, and I kept in contact with their parents and families. We were unique in what we did because most of the religious women in Bucharest taught in religious elementary and high schools. Those schools were excellent, but the poor did not attend those schools; we got our children from the public schools. The Sisters of Social Service covered all the catechetics for the public school children. We tried to do everything for these poor children. We organized trips and excursions so they would have fun.

The mission in Bucharest was started fifteen years before I arrived. Its original purpose was to respond to the needs of the poor Hungarian girls who had come from Transylvania to work as domestic workers in Bucharest.

It was important for these girls to receive help, because they were naive and not well educated. It was the same in other countries, too, when young girls ended up in big urban centers at the turn of the century; they were totally at the mercy of everyone. They were in danger morally and physically and were often exploited. To combat this, our Sisters started an extended ministry for those young girls to help them keep their faith and their roots since they had been totally uprooted. It was later that the catechetical work I participated in was started. I only spent four years in Bucharest.

Chapter Six

"On April the twenty-third when our turn came, three of us were arrested."

Similar to other Soviet-occupied countries, the Communist government began to oppress the churches in Romania. Of all the major religious affiliations, such as the Orthodox Church, the Greek and Latin Rite Catholic Churches and the Protestant Church, the government chose the Orthodox Church for preferential treatment, so long as the Orthodox Church agreed to accept State control and assume a position of servitude.

Next, the government pressured the Greek Rite Catholics to secede from Rome and to embrace Orthodoxy. In fact, the government decreed on December 2, 1948 that the Greek Catholic Church "shall cease to exist." In turn, all Greek Catholic properties were confiscated, and all bishops were arrested. The Greek Catholic clergy, too, was pressured to join the Orthodox Church; however, most chose to go into hiding in order to minister secretly to the faithful.

In July 1948, a decree subordinating the Latin Catholic Church to the State was passed. Yet, the government did not succeed in pressuring the Church to break off from Rome. With that, the Catholic Resistance Movement began. The Latin bishops protested the confiscation of schools, the closing down of Catholic hospitals and the suppression of religious orders. As a consequence of their protest, these bishops were arrested.

A year later, a decree dissolved all religious orders, effective as of August 15, 1949. And, on the night of August 15, police officials forcibly moved many members of the religious orders to a remote village and left them there. A few days later, the religious members were informed that they had three choices: to move into designated convents with State-approved superiors, register to work in State-controlled schools, or return home to their families.

The Sisters of Social Service's District Residence in Cluj was among the convents seized. As such, the Sisters were forcibly removed and transported to a small village. They found themselves without any means of existence. In the city of Bucharest, four of us Sisters and two novices were fortunate, because we were able to stay on where we lived.

With the nationalization of Catholic schools, all children attended public schools. This meant catechism was only possible through the parishes. For two years we continued our work in pastoral ministry. It was not explicitly forbidden, but the Communist officials watched us closely.

There was another factor. The plan of the Communists was to set up a Catholic Church that would no longer be connected to the Vatican. On July 7, 1950, the government expelled the Apostolic Nuncio of Bucharest, accusing him of espionage. Therefore, all official communication between the Church and Vatican ceased. Monsignor Del Mestri, secretary to the Nuncio, foreseeing this situation, appointed certain persons to maintain the relationship. Before leaving, the Nuncio consecrated, in secret, Monsignor Joseph Schubert to bishop, and gave him the task of mediating between the appointed persons and the Vatican. The Secretary of the Nuncio also included some of our Sisters in the mediating.

The relationship between the Sisters of Social Service and the Nuncio developed over the years, since Sister Hildegard Reissner was involved in the Catholic Relief Services after World War II.

Before leaving the country, Monsignor Del Mestri came to our convent. Sister Hildegard, because of poor health, was on vacation out-of-town. I took the assignment from him. It said that Hildegard, Christine and Judith should continue to maintain a relationship between the diocese and Bishop Shubert. We were to ensure, in case anyone was arrested, there would be other trustworthy persons willing to do the work.

In August 1950, we were awakened in the middle of the night by the Secret Police ringing our bell. When we answered the door, they rushed into the apartment. In a minute, they went through the rooms and saw that three beds had been slept in but only two women were present. They were convinced we were hiding someone. The reality, however, was that our novice, Bartholomea, was so scared she had run out the side door. The policemen would not settle for anything less than seeing her. They searched everywhere and everything.

Luckily, they did not find anything. They left an hour later. From that moment on, we did not have one quiet night. Each time a car stopped in front of the house, we thought it was the Secret Police. We were unable to overcome the fear we experienced that night, and we placed our novice in the home of a family to spare her.

In September 1950, we continued our catechetical work and took turns traveling to Alba Julia. We delivered messages to a Franciscan Father, who then transmitted them through the Italian Embassy to the Vatican. The responses from the Vatican came via the same route.

Each trip was full of danger. We learned that the dioceses were watched closely, and that we, too, were watched. We were sure that sooner or later we would be arrested, although we were not supposed to "know" anything. The Communists had a spy system in every embassy. With their recording machines, they found out everything. As such, it was soon discovered that the Church was continuing its relationship with the Vatican. All the priests who had replaced the arrested bishops were now arrested, as well.

On January 24, 1951, Bishop Schubert was arrested. Sister Hildegard continued her "activity of courier" undercover, dealing with an employee of the Italian Embassy. In March 1951, the Vicar of Alba Julia was arrested. The Vicar of Timisoara also was arrested, and so was our Sister Eva.

On April 23, our turn came. Three of us were arrested: Sister Hildegard, Sister Christine and I. At 12:20 a.m., we were awakened by the Secret Police. We knew that our hour had come. Sister Hildegard and I let in the police. They searched our bedroom. Then they showed me the order for our arrests, and told Sister Hildegard and me to get dressed and follow them. They allowed us to take a few things in a small suitcase. They even allowed me to take a blanket and sheet.

A car was waiting in front of the house. Darkness and quiet reigned as they blindfolded us. We were not allowed to communicate with each other.

We later learned that we were driven to the Ministry of the Interior and taken to the ground floor. That first night in prison, Sister Hildegard and I were separated from each other. We waited many hours before we were taken into an office and body searched. It was there I noticed Sister Christine's bag. This meant that she, too, was arrested from her residence at the rectory.

Chapter Seven

"I was really at peace because I had a deep conviction that everything had a purpose and suffering was not in vain."

The first night of my incarceration, I was registered. This meant I had everything taken away from me that I could have used to commit suicide, like shoelaces or a comb. I also was searched to see if I was hiding anything. I felt so violated.

This was just the beginning. I didn't see the other Sisters, but it seemed to me that they weren't too far away. I spent the night on a bench. In the morning, I was taken to an office for interrogation.

The Communist police had a method. They would tell you that you did this and you did that, and they would use information they extracted from those arrested before you. They also tortured prisoners. I found out that the priests were tortured, and some of them were unable to keep secrets, so they gave away information.

I was forced to write down what I said. My hand shook so much I could not write. It was the fear and terror; I didn't show it, but I was unable to control my hand. They shouted at me, "We know you did it! We know you did it!" I didn't acknowledge anything.

I was taken to a cell. It was underground and one wall was a full window that looked out to a corridor where a guard walked back and forth, constantly watching us. Each cell also had a door with something that could be opened from the outside, through which the guards watched us. They watched us from both sides. We were continually under their eyes in this high security prison.

There were two other women with me in the cell, but one was taken out right away. The other one I remember because we were together for a longer time, maybe two weeks. I don't know how many months she was there before I arrived. She talked to me about how she was tortured and about the system. She, too, was accused of espionage.

She happened to be a Jewish woman, who was a French and English teacher, and she had a little son. Her husband was not involved. Her name was Salome Benedict, and she was sentenced to twenty years.

I was later put in another, larger room with seven other women. This room didn't have the large window for them to watch us. I stayed there for a few weeks and was questioned many times. Each time I was taken out, I was blindfolded so I didn't know where I was going. When I entered the room in which I was questioned, the blindfold was removed. I was repeatedly asked what Hildegard and everyone else had done. At one point they told me exactly what I had done, and I realized there was nothing more I could do.

My great concern was that I not give them any information that could be used against anyone else. Once it was obvious that when under pressure, some people acknowledged certain things, I just tried to keep other people out of it.

I was there for six or seven weeks. Ultimately, I signed a confession, and they sent me to another prison where thousands of people were kept waiting for their trials or some decision. Jilava was a terrible place located on the outskirts of Bucharest. It also was underground and was built as a place to keep ammunition. The men were kept in one section and the women in another. The women were housed in only four rooms, but the rooms were huge. The floor was cement and there were two levels of wooden sleeping areas that contained straw mattresses. We were so crowded we had to sleep feet to head on one mattress. There was no toilet, only a barrel. There was another barrel filled with drinking water, but it was never enough for all of us. There was no shower. We used only one little container of water for washing. The food was extremely poor.

This is where we lived, and no one knew how long she would be there. I was there about three weeks before they took me to Ghencea. I did not know where I was, but at Ghencea, political prisoners were mixed with non-political prisoners. We waited to be sent to a labor camp, which was for people for whom they could not find sufficient reason to take to trial. It seemed as if I would not be tried.

I was then transported to a regular labor camp, where we lived in barracks. Every morning, hundreds of us lined up to work the whole day in the fields. Because they just wanted to keep us busy, we planted trees in December. We dug big holes. It was terribly cold. They gave us striped prison clothing and boots, but we were still cold. We walked an hour or two to get to the place, and then we worked extremely hard. Our group was women only, because men and women were not mixed. We also had women guards at this place.

This was, however, a place where prisoners were allowed to write home and ask for food or clothing. I wrote to someone in Salonta and once to the novice I thought was in Bucharest. I think I received one or two packages.

During the several months I spent at this labor camp, I got an infection on my leg and was very sick. My leg was all inflamed. I stayed in the barracks for a day or two, and then I worked again. They wouldn't let you die, but they did very little for you. After awhile, they realized I didn't have the energy to dig those holes, so they gave me another assignment. It was my job to carry a bucket of water and offer it to all the inmates. It was an easier job and it gave me the chance to talk to people.

One of the women I met, Colette Grossu, was imprisoned because of her faith. She was an associate of Pastor Wurmbrand, a Lutheran of Jewish background, who was extremely courageous. The Communists couldn't tolerate him, so they arrested him. The wife of Pastor Wurmbrand was at this camp, too. I still maintain contact with him and his wife.

In the evening, we stayed in the barracks where there was some heat and cold showers. We also were allowed to talk. Most people got packages and we shared with each other. It was in the spring when I was transferred during the night to Tirgusor. At this prison, we didn't work. I was placed in a huge room that contained three levels of beds and a thousand women. The prisoners were a mix of political and non-political; people were there for many different crimes. The atmosphere was very heavy. We didn't know why we were there or how long we would stay. We lived without knowing anything about what would happen to us. During the day, we tried to minister to, and care for, one another.

Through all of this, I was actually at peace because I had a deep conviction that everything had a purpose and the suffering was not in vain. I believed very much in the mystery of being united with Christ in his passion and participating in some mysterious way in His redemptive suffering. That was my vision during this whole time, and it gave me great peace. I never felt being in prison was meaningless. I also was grateful to be able to talk to people. I discovered there was a great hunger for God. Many discouraged and hopeless people, who did not see any meaning, hoped deep down in their hearts there was a God. They were searching for God. There may have been a time when they were believers, but they had forgotten about God. For many it was an experience of being stripped of everything and then discovering the experience of God. Many wanted to know more about God and wanted to pray more. We prayed whenever we could. In this big place it was possible because we were not watched as closely.

We did have to get up early — at five-thirty — even though we had no work to do. And the lights were left on all night. We discovered that during the night was a good time to get some water because most people used the water during the day. I was at Tirgusor for a couple of months.

In May 1952, I was taken alone in a car. Again, I did not know where I was being taken. We stopped in a city I recognized, but we only stayed the night. Then I was brought back to the Department of the Interior in Bucharest. I was kept in solitary confinement for two weeks, and I was interrogated again. Those two weeks were very hard. I was then put in another room with a Jewish woman who was accused of Zionism, which also was a crime. Zionists were actively persecuted in Romania at this time. The woman I shared that room with now lives in Israel, and we still correspond today.

Chapter Eight

"... I learned I was sentenced to ten years."

I was brought back to the Department of the Interior because that is where I was prepared as a witness in the trial of the bishops and priests. This incident stands out very much in my whole experience because it was so painful. It was a short trial, which forced the accused first to acknowledge everything, and then to be declared a spy and/or criminal.

It was 1952 when I was placed in solitary confinement and prepared to be a witness. It was a tortuous experience. I was to witness the trials of the other persons with whom I was involved. A long questioning period, during which I was obliged to answer different questions and write down the answers several times, preceded the trial. Only in retrospect did I realize that my answers came very close to the answers the police wanted to obtain.

When I was asked by a high officer the day before the trial whether I was compelled to these answers by torture or I was really convinced of my written statement, I confidently answered that I would never give a statement which did not correspond to reality, even if compelled by torture.

In looking back, I saw I was brainwashed and I didn't even realize it. They wanted witnesses to prove the Church leaders had committed espionage, and that is how they wanted me to testify. They tried to force me to write down that I carried letters containing political and military information. I was opposed to this and resisted writing it since it wasn't the truth. However, where I fell into their trap was when they told me they didn't need all that information, and it would be enough for me to say I had simply carried the letters.

I thought that acknowledging this would prove nothing. I didn't realize that by just publicly acknowledging I carried the letters, I supported their case. I was so naive; I didn't even know what it meant to testify against someone. I was willing to admit I carried the letters, but I was used to prosecute others.

The authorities wanted to make sure I was going to do what they expected of me. When they asked me what I was going to say, I answered with such assuredness. I told them I could never be forced to say something I did not do. But the day after the bishops' trials, when the interrogators were extremely friendly, I realized they used me. I suffered so much then, and I kept asking myself how I was unable to see what they were doing. But it was a fait accompli. I could not change it, and the painful thing was that I didn't have anyone with whom I could share this burden. I carried it all myself.

My testimony supported the accusations against Monsignor Schubert and the others. And since we worked and collaborated with them, we also were considered spies, but were not found as guilty as those who wrote and read the information that had come from the Vatican. Because we never saw the actual correspondence, we were considered lesser spies, who simply carried pieces of paper. But since everything was made to look political, they made it seem as if the letters contained political and military information. It was all made into espionage.

In October 1952, I was sentenced. It had been a year and a half since I was arrested. While I waited for my trial, I was placed again in Jilava. The sentencing involved another Sister and me. We both were found to be accomplices of those who committed espionage, and we were to be sentenced for the same thing. Under great secrecy, we were blindfolded and put into a van. When we got to court, the other Sister, Dorothea, and I recognized each other. We had lived together in Bucharest.

Later, the officials came, led us to an office somewhere in the prison, and read us our sentence. That's where I learned that I was sentenced to ten years. It was a shock; I couldn't have imagined that I would receive ten years. It was very hard to deal with the reality that this way of life would last so long. I wasn't told anything more — just that my sentence was ten years.

Shortly after that in the fall of 1952, Sister Dorothea and I were transported to Mislea where we would spend the term. Mislea was located in Romania proper, a few hours by train from Bucharest. It was a relatively big prison for women only. It looked like a more civilized place because it was a working prison and it contained dormitories. When we got up in the morning, we ate and then we went to the workshops. We were all political prisoners. Previously, Mislea was a regular prison, but it now was a women's prison for political prisoners.

There were two kinds of workshops in the prison. In one, we wove Persian carpets. It was very hard work. In the other workshop, we sewed using sewing machines. We mostly made men's shirts. I worked in both workshops, depending on where more workers were needed. There were times when we worked for twelve hours, from six to six, and then we slept for twelve hours. Then there were times when there were three, eight-hour shifts. We took turns – working sometimes in the night, sometimes in the morning and sometimes during the day. Always, very much was expected of us. We had to produce a certain quantity of rugs or shirts.

The conditions were very harsh. Nothing was electric, the machines broke down often and they were hard to push. We sat when we wove, and sometimes we had such huge carpets, eight of us worked side by side. In the beginning, I was not put on a sewing machine because some work needed to be done by hand. But after a while, I was put on the machines. In a way, I was glad to learn something and do something.

Making the carpets was extremely difficult. Some of the inmates worked quickly, and I admired how they did it. There were always people helping other people. For example, one woman who sat next to me worked so fast, that she took the larger part and left me the smaller part to complete. I knew through the help others gave that they were showing goodness. Basically, we had a great sense of solidarity with each other.

We were not restricted at Mislea and could talk to anyone, except for a group of prisoners in one section in a building. These prisoners did not have working privileges. The Communists viewed working as a privilege, and for many of the inmates, it was. Work allowed you to move around a little bit, and not to think about those at home and what might be happening to children and loved ones. Yet, the work and conditions were terribly harsh.

For a while, Sister Hildegard was in this restricted area, and so was another Benedictine Major Superior, Hildegardis Wulf OSB. They were restricted because they were more involved in the "crimes." Also in the restricted area were Annie and Nora Samuelli, sisters who became very important figures in my life. One of the sisters had worked at the American Embassy and the other at the British Embassy. After a while, Sister Hildegard was put in the section for those with tuberculosis.

I spent a few years at Mislea, and then, in 1956, during the Hungarian uprising, the Romanians became terrified an uprising would happen in Romania, so they closed the prison. They transported everyone to Csikszereda (Miercurea Ciuc) in Transylvania, where most of the guards were Hungarian. That's where I spent the next five years. I didn't work, I just lived in a cell with other people.

At Csikszereda, I spent a lot of time with Sister Christine, who had lived in the Hungarian parish in Bucharest. We stayed together in this prison, and she helped me with everything. She was wonderful and unselfish, a person who gave away everything she had. She also was blessed with good strength, and could eat whatever we were given. While she was practically never sick in prison, I was always sick and could not tolerate the food. We shared what we had. She gave me her little piece of bread, and I gave her what I couldn't eat. She carried the heavy barrels I couldn't carry. The primitiveness of the buildings was unimaginable. We had to carry our drinking water and barrels of waste up and down the stairs to and from our rooms. The barrels were so heavy, and Sister Christine did everything she could to make it easier for me.

There were bars and shutters on the windows. If you wanted to see the sky, you had to look through a small crack in the shutters. Every day, we were taken outside for a ten to fifteen minute walk. We walked in a circle under strict supervision because prisoners always figured out some way to get messages to each other. One way we sent messages if we learned something from a new inmate was to engrave notes on soap and then hide the soap under a stone or in the restroom where the waste was emptied. The women and men guards watched us closely, because communication was forbidden. If you were caught communicating you were punished severely. Your mattress was removed from your room, and you slept on the concrete for a few days. Punishments also meant being placed in a solitary cell with only water and bread or cornbread for five days. The guards really made it difficult for prisoners who broke the rules.

For a while, I was in a cell with about twelve women. Then I lived with twenty other prisoners, and after that, I was placed in a very large cell where I met the Samuelli sisters again. They had a wonderful gift for telling stories. They told us whole novels. They also taught us English.

Prisoners were moved around quite a bit, so I was never with the same people for too long. But no matter who I was with, we always taught each other. I gave meditations, taught French, and refreshed my German because there was a German woman there. I learned English, too; there was a little group who wanted to learn it, so I joined them. Everyone was happy to teach someone else.

I knew my ten years were almost up, but no one knew what happened to you when your sentence was finished. We heard that when some completed their sentences, they were sent to labor camps. The Communists didn't trust everyone to be free. For example, in all the prisons, there were inmates there for religious reasons, including lay people, as well as people who had worked at embassies, who were imprisoned for political reasons. There was another, larger group of so-called "Iron Guard," or the equivalent of fascists, who were a strong political group during the war. After the war, they all were arrested and thousands of them died in prison, especially the men, because they were considered the greatest enemies.

Most of the people who belonged to the Iron Guard in Romania mixed their political beliefs with their religious beliefs. They were believing people, but they were so brainwashed with the Nazi and fascist theory that they didn't see its inconsistency with their faith.

I was with many of these women and some were beautiful people. There was one with whom I spoke often, and her name was Viorica. These women were sentenced to many years of prison, and the husbands of many were in prison, too. They were tortured very much because the Communists never thought they caught all the Nazis. The Iron Guard was feared by everyone, but when you met these people in prison, they were just beautiful women with deep faith. They were all Greek Orthodox.

I wasn't sure if the officials would really set me free. No one was ever sure. I remember being questioned before I was released. The feelings I had at this time were very deep because I kept thinking, I'll be going home and all the others will be staying here another ten, fifteen or twenty-five more years. I was so heartbroken when I thought of Hildegard, because I knew she was close by. I took all kinds of chances to get to her cell door so I could say a few words to her. It was very difficult to know I was going to leave and she would stay. She was sentenced to eighteen years, but as it turned out, she didn't have to stay all that time because of the amnesty in the 1960s.

I really could not feel any joy at my liberation. When the guard came into the cell and said, "Take what you have here," and gave me my suitcase, I was numb. I didn't have much to pack, because when I was transferred from Mislea, my things were sent back to Bucharest. Later, I found out that when the Sisters received my belongings, they thought I had died. There was even a write-up in the newsletter of our American Sisters concerning my death.

I had very little to take with me when I left the prison. I had a skirt and a blouse and not much more. I was literally put out of the prison gates with nothing. Before I was released, I was asked where I wanted to go. I said Bucharest because that was where I was arrested. I had nowhere else to go. I was all alone.

I knew there was one of our Sisters living in the city where the prison was, but I had no idea where she lived. I do not know how, but I found her. When I knocked on her door, she couldn't believe it. Her name was Alberta, and she and the other Sisters were very loving and happy. They prepared a big meal to celebrate my freedom. After sharing that meal, I continued my trip to Bucharest where I had to register with the authorities. I went to the Hungarian parish and Sister Agatha was waiting for me. She waited for any of us who returned.

I stayed there for a year, but I never received permanent residence because the city was closed to ex-prisoners.

Chapter Nine

"... then I don't know why you freed me in the first place."

I wasn't relieved when I was released from prison because I was still living in prison in my heart. You reach a point where you are so united with the people you suffer with in prison, that even though you are out, in your heart, you continue to be with them in spirit.

Sister Augusta often came to visit me in Bucharest, and I will never forget how she risked her own safety to help me. The other Sisters tried to prevent her from coming to me, but she said she must go. Everyone who had connections with ex-prisoners was in danger, but that didn't matter to Sister Augusta. Whenever she came to see me, we cried. We were just so happy to be together. I can't recall any of our conversations, just Sister Augusta's great love and affection. She was in prison three times herself before she saw me.

Soon, I had to figure out what to do and how to take care of myself. I thought about what to do with my new freedom. At that point, I didn't realize how hard it would be to find a place to live and a job. I went to the police and reported, and I asked for permanent residence. The police told me to get a job and then come back and let them know. But when I went out into the real world, I realized no one would give me a job. However, I made some connections through Sister Agatha, with whom I lived in Bucharest. People heard that a Sister was home and they asked what they could do to help. Many of them were very nice. They wanted to express their love and compassion, so I received the basics I needed – food and clothing.

The Samuelli sisters I met and befriended in prison were ransomed, so they, too, were free. I got in contact with them. They invited me to their home and I met their mother. Soon after I saw them, the sisters began to make preparations to go to France. They asked what they could do for me. They wanted to make connections with our Sisters abroad to try and help me. They knew all about the Sisters of Social Service because they were with Sister Hildegard in prison, and at some point, with Sister Christine, also.

My first job was to take care of a woman who was dying of cancer. Just like in Romania today, there were no nursing homes and always a need for caregivers. Caregiving was the first thing I did because there was a need. I remember spending nights with this poor woman. It was heart-breaking.

I then got a job working for a professional couple. After Mass every day, I went to their house, did a little housekeeping and waited for their little boy to come home from school so I could take care of him. When summer came, they made arrangements for me to take care of their little boy at their summer home. In the fall we returned to Bucharest because the boy had to go to school.

Periodically, I reported back to the authorities and tried to get my residency permit renewed. The police only would give it to me for a few months at a time. I wondered how long I could live without a permanent residence permit. To help me, the Sisters in other cities started to suggest places where I could go. I wrote to these places only to find out that they also were closed cities. Where could I go? I would just have the same problems.

I kept trying, but nothing worked. I got more and more discouraged. I said to myself, "What is there for me?" Once I went to the police and said, "If there is no job for me, why don't you give me permission to leave the country?" And they said, "For you? We would never give you permission!"

To allow an ex-prisoner to leave the country was a privilege the police did not often grant – except if they were to receive money. I wasn't granted permission to live in Bucharest or anywhere else. I couldn't complain, though, because people were good and loving. I wasn't that lonely, but it seemed like an impasse; my life was at a dead end.

I decided to go to Cluj. I was given permission and told to report there. It was a big step, and I hoped it would be better because I would be back in Transylvania with the other Sisters. Yet, another problem arose.

In Cluj, I went to the police and they said they wanted me to give them information. I told them to put me back in jail. I said if I had no right to have a job or live in a certain place then I didn't know why they freed me in the first place. The police in Cluj realized I was not going to give them information. They told me to go to a small city or town and gave me some suggestions. I knew no one in the suggested areas, but some of our Sisters knew people in Gherla, so I decided to give it a try. It was close to Cluj, about forty minutes by train.

One day, I went to visit a family named Nitch who knew Sister

Augusta. They gave me the address of a very poor older woman. The family thought that perhaps I could help her. In all honesty, you could not imagine a woman who was any less likable. She was rather surly and difficult.

However, she was receptive to the idea that I live with her, but she did not have a regular apartment, only a single little room. This room contained her kitchen, bedroom and everything, and it was extremely primitive. She only had a sofa for me to sleep on, and there was no bathroom.

I tried to explore where else I might work in Gherla. The Nitch family introduced me to other people. Most of the Catholic people I met were Armenian. A large number of Armenians settled in Gherla about a hundred years earlier when they experienced persecution. They built a beautiful church and colony.

I was introduced to Dr. Frankel and his wife. He was a Catholic of Jewish background, and he and his wife became my best friends. In turn, he introduced me to the Lengyel family who was brought to Gherla forcibly because they were landowners.

The Nitch, Frankel and Lengyel families did everything they could for me. They tried to figure out where I could work, and they asked for help from everyone they knew. Finally, they connected me with a cooperative factory. The factory had a carpentry workshop, a Persian rug workshop and a few other workshops. When my friends asked me what skills I had so they could look for work for me, I told them about my work in prison making Persian rugs.

I was sent to a man who was not the director of the factory since he was not a member of the Communist party, but he was the totum factum there. He was the head of the accounting department for all the programs. He interviewed me, and was so touched by my story that he started to cry. He said he wanted to do something for me. He thought maybe he could place me in the rug workshop, but that he could give me a less taxing job than a weaver. Because the Communist system excluded ex-prisoners from white-collar positions, I couldn't be hired as white-collar worker.

I had to go through all the formalities, including asking the woman I lived with for a paper that verified I had a place to live. Finally, I was given permission to settle in Gherla. It was very difficult to find a job I could do and that the authorities would allow me to do. Originally, I was instructed to look for a laborer's job, and there was a farming program in that cooperative, but I was unable to do that kind of heavy work.

It took a few weeks, but I did get permission. I moved into the room with the old woman and began work. The rug factory was run by Armenians, who were very gifted rug-makers. My job was to work in the storage area where all the materials and supplies were handled. I was trained to store the supplies and to give out materials to the women working in the factory.

This was in the spring of 1962. It took me exactly one year to get a place to live and a job. I was grateful to receive a salary so I could pay the lady for the area in her room. We became friendly after a while.

I was still very heartbroken at this time, wondering what I was going to do with my life. At almost forty years old, I wondered if this was how I was going to spend the rest of my life. I felt so lonesome, terribly lonesome. I occasionally went to Cluj to visit the Sisters because it wasn't too far. That was wonderful. I got to spend time with Sister Augusta and some of the other Sisters.

The Nitchs, Frankels and Lengyels were always supportive of me. They invited me for Christmas, to spend Sundays with them, or to go out on excursions with them. But I was still lonely. I was pleased there were two Catholic churches in Gherla, one Armenian and one Roman Catholic, and I went to church every day. I prayed to know what God's will for me was.

This also was a time of experiencing the goodness of people in such a beautiful way. Marika Lengyel was extremely compassionate. She was like the St. Elizabeth of Gherla. She and her husband knew all the old people and all the sick people. They helped people, and they were good to everybody, not just to me. They constantly thought about how they could help me. At one point, Marika invited me every day for a meal. A few months later, she heard about a widow who was willing to take me in. I soon moved in with this woman.

This place was much better because I had my own room. I didn't have total privacy though, because the woman had to walk through my room to get to the kitchen. She was a very kind and religious woman, a Greek Catholic. It was more pleasant to live with her.

I developed some relationships with women at work, but my boss warned me not to try and preach to anyone. The factory owners knew I was a Sister, and they wanted me to know the limits. Everything was suspect. Once you were a political prisoner, you were always suspected of doing the wrong thing. The authorities imagined that I would talk about God or encourage people to go to church. I didn't do that, but that's what they imagined I would do.

I was terribly restricted, and I felt I didn't have permission to talk at all. I didn't know what to do. Even though I was free, I didn't feel any true sense of freedom. However, my boss always looked out for me. I liked him very much. He had so much compassion.

I was in Gherla for only one and a half years. Thanks to the intervention of the Samuelli sisters, who, after being ransomed by their relatives and given passports to France, moved every stone they could to help other inmates they knew.

The Samuelli sisters contacted Sister Natalie in America. She somehow managed to convey to the Sisters in Hungary that there was a way to get me out. The Nuncio of Bucharest, who was expelled in 1949, was now an American bishop – Bishop Gerald O'Hara. Once in the free world, he tried to do all he could to liberate us from prison. For many years it was impossible, but now he had an opportunity. I was the only one among the imprisoned Sisters who benefited from his efforts.

Through the Samuelli sisters, he learned about Romanian intentions to let certain people be "ransomed" by their relatives living in the West. I already was out of prison when Bishop O'Hara, then in London, intervened on my behalf. The Romanian government, which wanted all the foreign currency it could get through the ransoms, strongly encouraged me to apply for a passport. Sister Augusta got the word and asked me if I was interested in going to America. She knew we had Sisters there. There was some communication, but it was very dangerous. I thought about this opportunity, and I prayed about it a lot.

I asked some of the Sisters to ask the wise bishop of Alba Julia, Bishop Marton Aron, to give me advice. Word came from him that said, "By all means go if you can." I made the decision to go, but I did not know how these things worked.

Sometime in the summer of 1963, I got a notice from the government to report to Bucharest. I didn't know what the authorities wanted. When I reported, I was asked who I knew in America. The authorities always tried to scare you first. I didn't say anything about the Sisters. I told them only of my cousin. They asked where my cousin lived and I supplied her name and address. They asked if I wanted to go. I said yes, but that I was told a year earlier I couldn't go. They shouted, "Do you want to go or not?" Then they said, "Here are the papers; fill them out and return them in a half an hour if you want to go." I filled out the papers and applied for a passport. I then returned to Gherla.

At this time, many people already had been taken out of the country. And, when the entire ransoming scheme was made public in the Western world, it created a big scandal, but it had been going on for years. When family members managed to get out, they also paid for their relatives to get out. The government ran this process for years just to get foreign currency.

While I waited to hear back from the government, Sister Augusta encouraged me to visit the Sisters in Budapest. She knew they had more freedom than we did in Romania, and she knew I would enjoy being with them and sharing community with them. My experience in the early 1960s in Romania was mirrored by many other Sisters who were arrested and interrogated. We were constantly watched, and we had more Sisters in jail in Romania than anywhere else. In Romania, our Sisters, who bravely resisted oppression, were considered a minority group. Being considered minorities meant we were considered dangerous on two counts: for being Hungarian and Catholic. The Sisters in Hungary were better off. For example, in Budapest, a busy capital city, Sisters could peacefully gather in small groups.

I received permission to visit Hungary for a month. By 1963, my Uncle Alexander had died, but my Aunt Irene was still living. I visited her while I was in Hungary and she asked me to live with her because she was all alone. Her only daughter was already in America.

I stayed in Hungary for a month, and then I returned and continued my work in the factory. Sometime at the end of the summer, I received notice that I was approved for a passport. I couldn't believe it. I picked up my passport in Cluj, but my visa had to be picked up in Bucharest, where the embassies were located. I didn't know where to pick up my visa, and no one told me anything. There was no communication. I went to the same office I was at previously, and I asked where I could get my visa. No one there knew, so I was sent to the Austrian Embassy. It turned out, that at this same time, there was a mass action for Jewish people who wanted to leave Romania. For money, the government was going to let them go. The government workers thought my money was coming from Jewish sources, so I was sent to the Austrian Embassy, since that embassy was giving Jews a transit visa to Vienna. From Vienna, the Jews were then going to Israel. That's how I ended up at the Austrian Embassy. It was strange.

I was interviewed at the Austrian Embassy. When I was asked where I wanted to go, I said America, even though everyone else was going to

Israel. I received permission, and learned I would go to Vienna with all the other departing Jews.

On my way back to the Sisters' apartment in Bucharest, a secret policeman came up to me and threatened me. He said I could never leave unless I gave him all my jewelry and the deeds to any land I owned. The secret police did this to everyone who was granted permission to leave, because they wanted to seize everything. Maybe the Jewish people were trying to take some jewelry with them, but I had nothing to take. I told the police I had neither jewelry nor land.

This was a terrible time for me, because I already had given up my citizenship and I didn't know what I would do if I could not leave. I thought, "Who knows what they will do with me?" I had given up all my rights.

Ultimately, the Austrian Embassy provided me with my visa and also arranged for my plane ticket from Bucharest to Vienna, for which the Jewish organization paid. I left with only a suitcase of belongings. I left Romania with the hope of starting a new life. In a way, my leaving was like dying — but it carried the hope of a renewed existence. The Jewish organization had transportation waiting in Vienna, and we were taken to a hotel. I had an address for some Sisters in Vienna, and I made contact with them. Our Austrian Sister of Social Services, Sister Anastasia Kaiser, who lived in the beautiful mountains, also got in touch with me and helped me during my stay in Vienna.

Chapter Ten

"But somewhere deep in my heart was the hope that maybe I could begin a new life."

Somehow, I received word to call a certain phone number when I got to Vienna. It turned out to be the number of the Sisters of Charles de Borromeo. These nuns were asked by the Nuncio in Vienna to take me in when I arrived, so they were expecting me; Bishop O'Hara made the initial contact with the Nuncio. Some of these Sisters did housework for the Nuncio in Vienna, and they told him they would take me in when I arrived.

Within the hour of my calling, they came to the hotel. They immediately approached the Jewish organization, paid them back for the plane ticket, separated me from the group I had traveled with, and took me to the convent.

It was a convent with a nursing home for elderly people and there was a room for me there. Those Sisters were wonderful. I also met the priest who was in charge of the Nunciature. I was greeted with open arms and everyone wanted to know all about my experiences. These nuns instructed me about how I should report to the American Embassy and ask for asylum to the United States. All these arrangements had to be made through Sister Natalie, who was our Superior in America. She had to send papers and an affidavit that verified she would sponsor me. I had to go through the regular channels since I was applying as a political refugee. I spent four or five months in Vienna waiting for this process to be completed.

I kept very busy and soon learned of the Catholic Charities of Vienna. This organization wanted to learn all about the people who were suffering in Romania. I spent much of my time making contacts so I could send as much help as possible back to those who were in great need. I drew up lists of people to receive packages and money. I became a contact person for Transylvania because very few people in those years were able to come out.

The Catholic Charities of Vienna wanted to help, but didn't know how or to whom to send the aid. Representatives from the Catholic Charities of Munich came and interviewed me, so they, too, could learn about the conditions in Romania. I gave them information about my life and the people of Romania. I wrote many reports.

I started to correspond with our Sisters in America, and I sent letters to Romania. I also spent some time sight-seeing in Vienna. On one of my trips, while waiting in line, I met a woman named Johanna Beck. She was a single woman, and not a Catholic, but when she heard my story, she started to cry. We became good friends. She told me she had loved someone very, very much, but he was of Jewish background and she lost him.

Johanna Beck was an extremely spiritual and special person. She became my sponsor and took me to many places. She wanted me to have a beautiful time. I kept in touch with her when I came to America, and each time I went back to Europe, I visited her.

In Vienna, I did not live in the cloistered part of the convent, but instead had a room on the floor with the elderly people. I went to Mass in the Sisters' chapel, but I led my own life. To prepare for going to the United States, I practiced some English. It was a time of waiting.

Getting to Vienna was so unbelievable, and experiencing freedom was such a contrast to where I had come from, that I suffered terrible cultural shock. For days and weeks as I walked on the streets of Vienna, I just couldn't believe it was possible to live this way while other people were still in jail. I was so deeply united with the people I left, that I just couldn't forget them. I remember I was brokenhearted in a way because everywhere I looked I saw an abundance of freedom, and of people not worrying about anything, but I could only think of the people I left behind.

I thought of what I could do for the people who were still imprisoned. In a sense, I was living in the past. I also felt very lonely. In Romania, I had many friends and Sisters, but in Vienna, I was all by myself. The Sisters I lived with were very nice, but still, it wasn't the same thing. For me, it was a time of deep suffering, inner tearing apart, and wondering what was going to be. At the same time, I also thought that perhaps now I would be able to live out my mission. I thought that maybe I could start a new life in the hope that something good would happen. It was a very critical time, because the year before in Romania, I questioned my ability to live out my vocation and to be faithful to my call. I had at times felt hopeless with no ministry and no community.

In Vienna, I had a vague sense of hope, but I wondered what I would do in America. I thought "Who needs me there? What kind of ministry will I do in a country known as the land of plenty?" I had no concept whatsoever of what was awaiting me there. Nobody knew. Our Sisters in Romania couldn't tell me anything. It was like jumping into the dark. But some-where deep in my heart was the hope that maybe I could begin a new life.

During my stay in Vienna, I came across a poem, "The Hound of Heaven," by Francis Thompson. I immediately recognized myself in it. That poem represented the journey of my own life. God was always there, prompting me to search for the meaning of what was happening to me and around me, and inviting me to respond to the call of the moment…creating me anew and liberating me a thousand different ways.

PART II

A new Life.
A renewed Church.
A recreated Community.

I will create a new heart in you,
I will breathe a new spirit into you.
(Ezekiel)

In Part II (1964-2000) Judith shares her life in the United States, her challenges and opportunities, and her integral involvement with the renewal of the Sisters of Social Service, locally and abroad. This section shows how one person's spirit brings hope to others, near and far.

Chapter Eleven

"I became more and more convinced... that social work was a way in which our community could work with people who were not part of the mainstream."

1964-1968

I came to America fraught with all the anxiety and fear that so many immigrants before me experienced. Although I knew some English from what I learned from inmates in prison, I recognized that fluency would be a challenge. Yet, there was a feeling of joyful anticipation about the new freedom I had not known in my previous life. I remember when I was asked to speak at a retreat shortly after arriving in America, I explained why this freedom was so precious to me. I shared that the Church missed many chances to address the needs of the people. This gave the Communists the opportunities to delude people into believing that Communism would provide an "earthly paradise." I never wanted this to happen again. I hoped the United States and the American Church would take all the opportunities available to create a just and good life for all people. I deeply desired to be a part of the struggle for social justice for all.

I questioned, however, how I would fit in, what I would do, and how I would adjust to a country of plenty. I did not have the answers, but I knew I wanted to take every opportunity to develop myself, and I hoped in some way to affect the events in this new society. How could we influence further harmony among all races, to offer true brother/sisterhood and freedom for all? What would be the means to eliminate forms of oppression and inequality? These burning questions stayed with me.

When I arrived in Buffalo, the Sisters were extremely welcoming and I looked forward to creating new friendships and sharing in our communal life. I soon found this would not be so easy. The Sisters in America suffered through poverty, loneliness and extremely difficult work situations, and had little help with developing their language skills, as well as minimum opportunities to study. Because our community was so poor, the Sisters had to work, and in some ways, they felt used. They did not have the chance to become a part of American life, and they felt disengaged from its culture, which left them feeling alienated and disoriented. They felt so overwhelmed coping with their own situations; I soon realized that their resources to help me with my adjustment were limited. To see them feel displaced and undervalued broke my heart.

In addition, I was given the chance to be educated and this was an opportunity they did not share. It is difficult to be made the exception. Fortunately, with the passage of time, relationships formed, and gradually we came to know, respect and love each other. I felt very grateful to the Sisters, especially for all they did to relieve me from many community responsibilities that made it possible for me to concentrate on my studies. Friends outside of the community also were treasured supports. My professors, as well as others I met at meetings or gatherings, encouraged me and gave me new confidence. Sister Augusta's letters from Romania were lifelines.

In those early days, America reaffirmed my belief in the fullness of life and Jesus' words resonated in my heart, "I have come that they may have life and have it in abundance."

As head of the community, Sister Natalie was very anxious for me to begin my education. The Grey Nuns of the Sacred Heart at D'Youville College were very supportive of our small community from the beginning of our American existence. They continually offered scholarships for us to be educated in this country, and I became one of their college graduates. I began my studies at D'Youville College in 1964, the same year the Sisters moved to Linwood Avenue in the City of Buffalo. I stayed on the third floor and went back and forth to college from our home every day.

For ten years, while I was prison, any intellectual enrichment was inaccessible to me, so I thirsted for knowledge and delved into my studies. Two writers who deeply touched me during this time were Teilhard de Chardin and Victor Frankl.

I first encountered Teilhard de Chardin's writings in one of my philosophy courses. His life and vision fascinated me. I resonated deeply with his view of the universe as a vast, living organism in which human beings belong as an integral part. Teilhard integrated the theory of evolution with his own vision of Christianity — a fire with a vision of divine mystery at the heart of the cosmos. He was a prophet in the dialogue between religion, science and mysticism. His thoughts expanded my world and gave me a new sense of the sacred. This sacredness was something I always felt, but now it was articulated.

Another significant discovery came in a psychology course, where I learned about Victor Frankl's writings and his logotherapy. A survivor of several World War II Nazi death camps, Frankl, a Jew, realized that it was his very great love for his wife and the hope to be with her again that enabled him to go on in the midst of the most horrible circumstances. Logotherapy grew out of his own experiences as a way of helping people in crisis to find meaning in their lives, thereby enabling the human being to transcend the absurdities of life's circumstances. One can "survive" if there is openness for the future, if one can perceive a "task" waiting for them.

Frankl's theory shed light on the tragic moments of my own life and on my own survival. I recalled the devastation I felt in my heart when I realized that despite all my attempts to save them, my mother, two sisters and grandmother were deported. No words can describe what I experienced. I was not sure I could bear the pain. And yet, at a deeper level, I felt a light emerging.

I felt in the depth of my being that God, who is LOVE, would not abandon my beloved mother, sisters and grandmother. God's love is everlasting. I began to see it as my special task to support my loved ones – wherever they were – with my own life.

I also found strength in praying that all the suffering of my loved ones would be a source of life for them. Expanding this to include the sufferings of all others who experienced the horrors of persecution also became part of my task.

At the same time, a very deep longing grew in my heart for a world of love, justice and goodness. I envisioned this new world as being brought about by the sufferings endured by the innocent victims of unjust systems. My call to follow Christ gradually became a call to offer my entire life for living out the mission that was His: "I have come that they may have LIFE, and have it more abundantly."

One of my sociology professors at D'Youville College, Dr. Atanas Musteikis, encouraged me to write about my prison experience. For his courses, I wrote two papers. The first was entitled, "Personality Modifications Associated with Enforced Role Prescriptions as Observed among Political Women Prisoners in Communist Romania during 1951-1961."

This writing helped me to reflect upon what the prison experience meant to me. I was grateful to understand my years in prison in light of some sociological theories. I learned a lot about how people react in prison and in other situations of extreme stress. I learned more about relationships between inmates and authorities, and what people need to survive and to maintain their integrity in such situations. Eventually the paper was published as a pamphlet called *Women Prisoners Behind the Iron Curtain*, and it was distributed throughout the country.

A second paper that helped me to reflect on my past experience was entitled, "The Process of Liquidation of Religious Communities, As an Aspect of the 'Cultural Revolution' in Communist Romania (1948-1963)."

Through my classes, I also began to learn about the minorities living in America who were not part of the mainstream. I became very interested in this area of study. We studied current social problems: poverty, social institutions, and what the profession of social work was attempting to do about these issues.

I became more and more convinced through my courses and studies that social work was a way our community could work with people who were not part of the mainstream. It was an important realization for me. D'Youville College was my first window into American social situations.

These years were extremely enriching both intellectually and culturally. I was highly motivated to learn about what was going on in this country. I searched for my future ministry. I probed for a deeper understanding of the American culture and what the Sisters of Social Service might be able to offer the people of this country. My studies gave me insight into how we could minister to the people of the New World.

Community Life
Along with being devoted to my studies at D'Youville, I also was very

involved in the life of our community. During these years, our Advisory Board suggested ways to implement our vision in this country. The community was very interested in developing programs that would involve young people. We desired to share our vision, as well as our understanding of social awareness, with young people.

From 1965-1967, I coordinated the Social Service Volunteers, which was comprised primarily of high school students, although college students also participated. During monthly Sunday meetings, we talked about ways to relate to people who were in any kind of need. We also had days of prayer. We encouraged the young people to think of an area of interest to them, like working with children, visiting St. Rita's home where children with special needs resided, visiting the elderly in the Erie County Home and Infirmary, and/or teaching home economics to minority children.

Each group was assigned a Sister who was intensely involved and who accompanied them on the project. Even though my main responsibility was to study, I was very happy to interact with these young people and to share with them my interest and desire to make a difference.

Although we would have been happy if any of these young women wanted to join our community, the Sisters of Social Service believe that lay people hold an important role in our mission, and that just opening these young hearts was a valuable contribution. Interestingly, some of these young people did choose social work as a career.

Before I earned my degree, I was very inspired by the head of the social work faculty at D'Youville, Jeanette Costantino. Jeanette, and her husband, Carl, who also was a social worker, were excellent role models because they helped me get a good sense of what social work was all about in this country. Jeanette inspired me with her great understanding of social work and encouraged me to pursue a master's degree in the field. It was people like Jeanette Costantino who strengthened my resolve to meet my goals.

In 1966, I received my Bachelor of Arts degree in sociology with a minor in psychology from D'Youville College. I recognized my need for more learning, so I applied to graduate school. After a process of applying, gathering recommendations and writing an autobiographical statement, I was accepted in the Social Work Department at the State University of New York at Buffalo (UB).

Since social work was central to our community's charism, Catholic Charities of Buffalo offered our Sisters scholarships, if we then worked for them after we got our degrees. I was able to pursue a Masters of Social Work with financial assistance from Catholic Charities. In return, I agreed, upon completion of my degree, to work for their agency as a social worker for a minimum of two years.

Graduate Work

In the first year of my graduate program, my field placement was with the Urban League. I had the opportunity to work with African-Americans and to understand the tragic fate of this population, as well as some of the forces that prevented their integration into the mainstream of American society.

I identified with the alienation of the African-American population, considering my own Jewish minority background. Here, I felt there was another group of people who were not given access to resources and were stigmatized because of an incidental difference, the color of their skin.

I was grateful to be sensitized to the struggles, needs and aspirations of these people and to more deeply enter their lives. I felt even more strongly that, as Sisters of Social Service, we had a special mission in this country to minority people, just as our Foundress Sister Margaret led us to help the Jewish people in Eastern Europe. I, myself, personally experienced what a difference it made when people had the courage to become involved and to take risks for the sake of others. I could relate deeply to my work in this field placement.

At the time of my placement, Mary Frances Danner, who turned out to be a very dear friend in so many ways, was working at the Erie County Department of Social Services. The student unit to which I belonged, together with the County Social Service Department, established a program for single African-American mothers. It was a very collaborative project. I was much involved with the referrals, and we set up a program where we met with the young Aid to Dependent Children (ADC) mothers. We developed interest sheets and provided many enriching experiences for them.

I learned a great deal about group work by participating in the mothers' group. A wonderful African-American student in her second year of studies, Miss Walker, modeled for me many facilitation skills needed by a group leader. I was grateful to work with her.

I also became acquainted with other community resources and people, like outreach programs and welfare workers. I appreciated learning the history of the Urban League and how it worked to promote integration of

Sister Judith's mother, Elizabeth Fenyvesi (nee Waldmann),
and father, Francis Fenyvesi.
Below: Grandmother Jcny Fenyvesi, 1925.

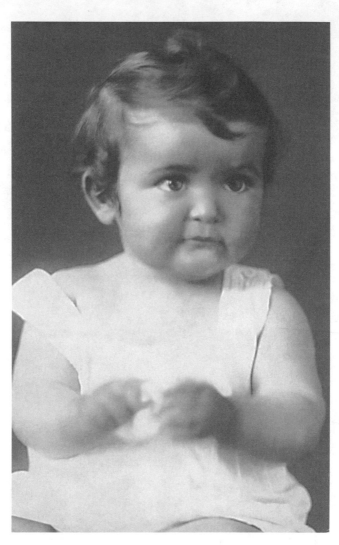

Judith, age 1, 1924.

Sister Margaret Slachta, 1929. Foundress of Sisters of Social
Service and first woman member of the Hungarian Parliament.

Fenyvesi sisters, 1929: Marta, age 5; Marianne, 8; and Judith, 6.

Francis Fenyvesi's pharmacy, Salonta, Romania, 1928.

Fenyvesi family, 1929.
Mother, Elizabeth and father, Francis.
Marta, age 5; Marianne, 8; and Judith, 6.

Sister Augusta, 1935, founding member of the
Sisters of Social Service and Provincial Superior
of the Transylvania District.

Mother, Elizabeth; father, Francis; and Judith, age 13, 1937.

Fenyvesi sisters, 1939,
at boarding school,
Notre Dame de Sion.

Marta, age 15;
Marianne, 18; and
Judith, 16.

Sister Rodica, Sister
of Notre Dame de
Sion, 1939. She was
an inspirational
source during Judith's
student years.

Judith, age 26, 1949.

Nora Samuelli, Sister Margaret Mary, and Sister Judith, 1965.

Sister Hildegard
and Monsignor
Schubert shortly
after their release
from prison.

Dr. Manzella and family, 1971.
Louis, Donna, James (in tree), Paul, John (seated), Anthony, Jr. (in tree),
Theresa, and Anthony.

Sister Judith,
1975.

Below:
Sister Angela,
Council Member,
SSS; Sister Anne,
General Moderator,
SSS; and Sister
Judith, Assistant
General
Moderator,1976.

Sister Judith at Auschwitz Concentration Camp, Poland, July 1983.

American Red Cross Letter, 1996, which states:

"Marta Fenyvesi was transferred on August 14, 1944 from Concentration Camp Auschwitz to Concentration Camp Stutthof and died there on January 14, 1945.

Elizabeth Fenyvesi, nee Waldmann, was transferred on August 14, 1944 from Concentration Camp Auschwitz to Concentration Camp Stutthof and died there on December 19, 1944.

We regret to inform you that no information is available about the other two persons for whom you are searching."

Sisters of Social Service, 1996

Sister Judith celebrates 50 years (Golden Jubilee) as a
member of the Sisters of Social Service, 1997.

Motherhouse of Sisters of Social Service located at 440 Linwood Avenue, Buffalo, New York. Sister Judith lived here from 1964 - 1999.

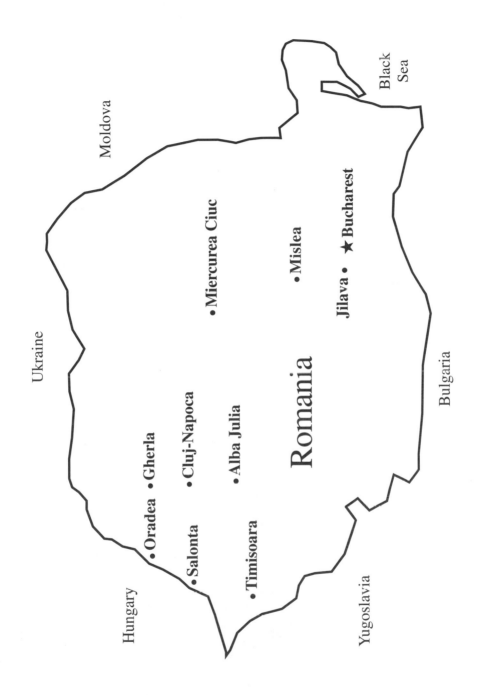

Organizational Structure of the Sisters of Social Service (SSS)

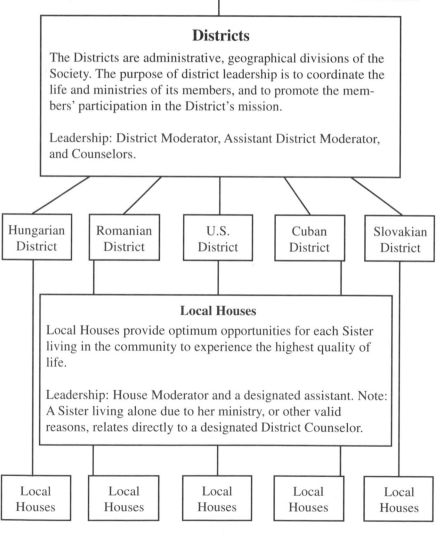

Generalate

The Generalate is the highest governing body of the SSS community. Its responsibility is to oversee the operation of the Districts, and to call the SSS community to fidelity to the Gospel, the SSS charism, and the apostolic needs of the times, thus enabling each Sister to fulfill her mission of service to the Church and secular society.

Leadership: General Moderator, Assistant General Moderator, and General Counselors.

Districts

The Districts are administrative, geographical divisions of the Society. The purpose of district leadership is to coordinate the life and ministries of its members, and to promote the members' participation in the District's mission.

Leadership: District Moderator, Assistant District Moderator, and Counselors.

Hungarian District | Romanian District | U.S. District | Cuban District | Slovakian District

Local Houses

Local Houses provide optimum opportunities for each Sister living in the community to experience the highest quality of life.

Leadership: House Moderator and a designated assistant. Note: A Sister living alone due to her ministry, or other valid reasons, relates directly to a designated District Counselor.

Local Houses | Local Houses | Local Houses | Local Houses | Local Houses

African-American people into the mainstream. This field placement was an awakening, and it encouraged me to continue to work with the African-American community.

This also was when the Church became involved with healing race relations. I became very much involved in this process, and learned what was developing in Catholic circles and among religious communities in the area of race relations.

The Challenge of Cancer

It was at this time in 1967, while still a graduate student, that I learned I had breast cancer. I first discovered a lump on my breast after I was released from prison, and Sister Augusta arranged for me to have a medical examination with a doctor in Budapest. The doctor assured me that it was nothing to worry about. Given this assurance, when the lump returned after I came to the United States, I didn't feel concerned.

But then I heard about a woman professor who discovered a lump that turned out to be cancerous. I decided to have my lump examined by our family doctor. He was alarmed with what he found and I was immediately hospitalized for surgery.

I felt very disappointed, because my schooling and field placements were going so well. However, that disappointment was nothing compared to facing a mastectomy, which was one of the most devastating experiences I ever endured. I simply could not adjust to the thought of being mutilated in that way. I thought I would rather die than go through this horror. There was no alternative; I understood the surgery was necessary.

Yet during this very difficult time, I experienced again God's tender love for me. Dr. Anthony Manzella, my surgeon, was extremely sensitive to my feelings and somehow helped me to accept myself as a whole person, in spite of the mutilation. I felt his genuine concern for me as a person, and I was consoled and grateful. This crisis was the beginning of a wonderful friendship that has lasted throughout my years in Buffalo. My relationships with Dr. Manzella, his dear wife Theresa, and their beautiful children, have been a continual source of special and deep joy in my life.

Perhaps other women would not have reacted so strongly to this surgery, but this was not my experience. After facing so many challenges in my life, some people found it strange that this affected me so profoundly, but it did. It was a question of the loss of my own physical integrity; I could not think of myself as complete. I found it extremely painful to look at myself. In some ways, losing a breast is a singularly lonely experience for a woman. I grieved over my loss, and I wondered how I could ever accept this condition, but the healing of my body and my spirit came. It was only a matter of time. This experience taught me to be more aware and sensitive to the handicaps of others. I started to realize recovery would give me the chance again to love.

I also was aware there were still many things I could accomplish for my own growth and that of my Sisters. I felt a renewed gratitude for another opportunity for life, and thankfulness to everyone who helped me through this illness. The Sisters in Buffalo prayed earnestly for me. In their frequent letters, Sister Augusta and Sister Lidia in Romania continued to assure me that they were very much with me in prayer and in their hearts. Friends I made outside of the community continually inquired with concern and love. One of these friends, Sister Margaret Mary Bradley, was desperate with worry. She communicated frequently with Dr. Manzella and later became friends with both him and his wife. I was eventually told that there was no metastasis.

As in other trials, I was surprised at how even a small thing could sustain me. My days of recovery might have been much harder if not for one special quote Sister Margaret Mary sent me: "I wake at dawn with a winged heart and give thanks for another day of loving." These words anchored my hope and renewed my gratitude. I realized that no matter what my condition, if each day I could awake knowing that this new day was another opportunity to love, my life would have meaning.

After the surgery, the professors and the students in my program at the university also showed great concern for me. During my early recovery, one teacher even arranged that our classes be held in our convent living room on Linwood Avenue. In this way, I could keep up. As soon as I was able, I returned to my regular class schedule at UB. After a few months, I also returned to my field placement at the Urban League.

Seeing Welfare from a New Perspective

I continued to be intensely involved with the Aid to Dependent Children mothers, both with individual clients and through group work. Since Miss Walker had completed her field work, I now had the responsibility of facilitating the group. This allowed me to experience the importance of facilitation skills.

The idea for the group was for the women see themselves in a new way, as being capable and motivated. The group became its own authority. No one from the outside told the mothers how to solve their problems. They shared their own wisdom, and the women learned to trust each other. They were frank and honest.

In fact, one group discussion topic was the young mothers' criticism of the Welfare System on which they relied for economic help. They expressed their distrust of the Welfare System. They saw the system as humiliating and controlling. The way the Welfare System was structured, the system knew everything that went on in a woman's life. The women shared the sense of shame and the stigma they felt. It wasn't a question of individual Welfare workers but of the system itself.

We did not want to jeopardize the clients' financial support, so we had continual discussions with the Welfare Department about how such a group would be assured of its freedom and autonomy. It was a question of a more humane approach to human beings.

The underlying perception Welfare imposed was the question of who was deserving and undeserving. The women felt a sense of shame, even though they were people who just couldn't make it without support. They also felt affected by Welfare's attitude that clients are dishonest and trying to cheat. All these experiences gave me a sense of meaning and mission.

My Sisters' Challenges

The longer I was in Buffalo, the more I realized that most of the Sisters who came before me were put in a position to work twenty-four hours a day with little time or energy left for education or self development. Opportunities to develop their talents and abilities, so needed for ministry to this country, were not available or offered. The Sisters couldn't see how they could contribute because they were not free to adapt to their new culture. This saddened me. Without exposure to the language and the people, the Sisters felt they could not integrate themselves into American life. They did not see their future here. In this "new world," they found little meaning, and even less hope that they would thrive here living in a religious community.

They were deeply convinced of our Foundress, Sister Margaret Slachta's vision, and searched for ways to make it a reality in the context of their lives, but they didn't believe it would be possible. In my great desire to respond to their reality, I wrote another paper, "An Analysis of the Society of the Sisters of Social Service in Historical Perspective

(1923-1968)." This paper expressed our community's vision.

One significant way we sought to reclaim the community's vision for the Sisters who felt unconnected and discouraged, and for the community as a whole, was through efforts to integrate the new theology and the message of the Vatican II Documents into our lives. We had regular spiritual readings and meetings to study the documents. We attended lectures and read analyses of the documents. We desired to discern what Vatican II meant to our community, and how our community would live out the vision of the Council. How could our community contribute while being faithful to our original charism*? I began to look at the injustices in this country and I saw ways in which, in the light of our charism, we could address some of the burning needs of our new country. I looked at the intrinsic value of each Sister and hoped through our charism, each would find ways to explore her unique and beautiful life to serve the American people and our community.

*charism: here, and in the following, refers to the extraordinary gift our Foundress and the community received from the Spirit to respond to particular needs manifested in a certain time of history to help address issues in the Church and in society.

Chapter Twelve

"With our small number and our status as immigrants with various experiences and facilities with English, the Sisters of Social Service had a daunting challenge."

1967-1970

In 1967, during my second year of graduate studies at the University of Buffalo, I wanted an experience in community organization, because mobilizing communities to work on their significant issues was part of the mission of the Sisters of Social Service. I believed it was important to work on this dimension of social work, especially since I had engaged in casework during my first year of study.

My advisor, Professor Caryl Fonda, a person with great sensitivity to minority people, felt the Commodore Perry Project would give me good experience in community organization. I worked at St. Brigid's parish with Father Sweeney, who was deeply committed to African Americans. My responsibility was to explore the different community groups functioning in this urban area. I also was involved with several families.

Another big societal issue happening during that time was school desegregation. I researched and wrote a paper on "The Issue of Desegregation in the Public School System of Buffalo and Catholic Attitudes Relative to It."

I also wrote my thesis for my Masters during this second year. It was entitled, "Nuns in a Low Income Housing Project: Aggiornamento at St. Brigid's." At the time, there was a movement in religious congregations in the United States to encourage Sisters to move into the ghetto to identify and live with the poor. The Mercy Sisters had already moved into the project, and I thought we, the Sisters of Social Service, should explore this possibility. The Advisory Board supported me. I would have liked to have done it, but none of the other Sisters were able to join in.

A Social Worker at Catholic Charities

Upon graduating with my M.S. in social work in July 1968, I was grateful to be hired by Catholic Charities as a social worker in the Parish Programs at Our Lady of Sorrows and at St. Mary Magdalene. Both of these parishes were going through transitions as I began to fulfill my two-year obligation as repayment for the master's degree tuition grant Catholic

Charities had provided.

In short, many families of Western and Eastern European origin were moving out of the two parishes' neighborhoods and African Americans were moving in. I was to work with the pastor, Catholic Charities personnel, individuals, and families.

During my studies, I tried to move beyond the casework and into community organization, the social work model that encourages people to mobilize for group empowerment on issues of importance to them. It was something I believed in, and it was a great challenge for me. In my new job, I became involved with several community groups.

The following January, my six month probationary evaluation indicated that my job performance was going very well, both in my personal style and in my professional commitment. For example, my evaluation stated: "This ability to get along with people helps make her a 'natural' in working with people." And, "In Our Lady of Sorrows, the needs are met more with the casework method; in St. Mary Magdalene, the Community Organization method is used more extensively. Sister is very competent in both."

As a result of the evaluation by the Diocesan Director of Catholic Charities, Monsignor John Coniff wrote a letter to welcome me to the regular staff. He wrote, "In four years of reading evaluations, this is the most glowing report I have ever seen of any worker in any part of the Catholic Charities organization. Sister, you are not only an excellent addition to our staff, but also an outstanding example to the other members of the organization. You are making a wonderful contribution to Catholic Charities and to the image of the Sisters of Social Service. We are delighted to have you and look forward to many years of happy association."

I felt confident of my relationship with Catholic Charities and never imagined the crisis I would face there the following year. But, at least for that time, my work was going well. I also was very interested in working with our community, which wanted to become more proactive in providing an expanded vision of its role.

In April 1969, our Advisory Board and the community commissioned me to do an in-depth research project on volunteer organizations whose aim it was to involve youth in social action. This was part of an Urban Ministry. The Advisory Board suggested that a Sister with a master's degree work full-time on this project. Although that was not possible, I requested spending one day a week on the Sisters of Social Service's Urban Ministry. Monsignor Coniff granted my request.

Through her connections at Maryknoll, Sister Margaret Mary Bradley set up a number of interviews with agencies in New York City, so I could understand what was needed to develop a volunteer youth social action group. From April 29 to May 4, 1969, Sister Margaret Mary accompanied me on a whirlwind tour of several active volunteer organizations in the New York City environs. We met many knowledgeable leaders and learned a great deal, which I reported to the Board. I saw many ways people in New York City worked with the poor, and I came back with ideas to invite young people to participate in a volunteer initiative.

During this time, I also prepared for the 1969 Chapter meeting, which I attended as a delegate of the Romanian District. Shortly after I came to the United States in 1964, Pope Paul VI, in his 1966 Encyclical, *Ecclesiae Sanctae: The Decree on the Adaptation and Renewal of Religious Life*, urged religious institutes to engage in a process of renewal.

Initially, the leadership of our community thought that this call for renewal did not apply to us because our Constitution was approved in 1966 by Bishop McNulty, the Bishop of Buffalo, New York. However, when consulting with the Sacred Congregation, we were informed that since the approval preceded the promulgation of *Ecclesiae Sanctae*, we, too, were obliged to hold a chapter of renewal.

As for all religious communities, the question of renewal was challenging, but perhaps for us even more so. With our small number and our status as immigrants with various experiences and proficiencies in English, the Sisters of Social Service had a daunting challenge.

During this time, some of us tried to research what the Church understood by "aggiornamento" and what it meant to us. We immersed ourselves in reading and consulting, while at the same time we hoped our leadership would ultimately agree that we needed to hold a special General Chapter (a gathering of the leadership and representatives from each district) to review what had occurred since the last Chapter, and to formulate the direction of the community for the upcoming years. Our Chapter addressed many concerns: formation of new members, leadership, spirituality, community, and ministry, as well as the cultural, political, religious, economic, and social conditions/problems of each country our districts represented, in order to promote solidarity with each other. An enormous amount of research and pre-planning was needed to have the most comprehensive and enlightened experience of our society and to prepare for the next six years of living out our charism.

The Chapter of 1969

By the time the 1969 General Chapter commenced, I had spent five years in the United States. I came to know the members of the American Sisters of Social Service, and I was rooted in this community group. This meant I had ample opportunity to experience the frustrations, as well as the longings, of the Sisters. I suffered with them, and I constantly reflected on the reality in which we lived, asking the question, "Where does God call us?" I was anxious to be part of the exploration of this question as a member of the Chapter.

I immersed myself in this work and was in charge of the position paper on the Apostolate. I used information from a questionnaire that I prepared for the Sisters to write proposals for the purpose of discussion at the Chapter.

The 1969 General Chapter was held at our Linwood Avenue house in Buffalo. During my preparation for the Chapter and during its session, Sister Teresina, who was working on her master's degree in Social Work at the time, took over my employment responsibilities at Catholic Charities.

In attendance were delegates from the Districts of Hungary and Romania, and sub-Districts of Slovakia, Cuba, and the United States. Each District was expected to report on the highlights of the six years since the last Chapter, held in 1963 in Buffalo, where Sister Natalie was elected the General Superior of the Sisters of Social Service.

In 1963, when Sister Natalie began her first term, there were many issues that needed to be addressed. She saw it as her task to guide the community in the spirit of Sister Margaret, to make Sister Margaret's teachings available to all, to obtain approval for our Constitution, to work for the establishment of the Motherhouse in Rome, and to develop the U.S. sub-District.

My hope for the 1969 Chapter was that we would very seriously consider all the recommendations of *Ecclesiae Sanctae*, and make use of this great opening up begun by the Vatican II Council. I hoped we would move in the direction of a full, more inclusive participation of all our members. It was a way to bring hope to our Buffalo Sisters.

This idea of collegiality, or full participation of all members, caused resistance that became apparent during the Chapter meetings. There were some differences in opinion on how we should make changes, as well as look at the original inspiration of our community and the signs of the times. Overall, changes were to be considered in light of Vatican II's *Document on the Constitution of the Church*. Our mission was to open up as a community and become a vital part of the Church's renewal.

As a consequence of the differences in opinion, a decision for full renewal did not come about; yet, there were many positive outcomes. Unfortunately, the implementation of these outcomes proved to be a great challenge. However, Sister Margaret, our Foundress, was our champion. Our community history was filled with opportunities to work for change, and to bring a deeper involvement of every member into the creation of our communal life and mission. Sister Margaret fought for the rights, value and voice of each person. We believed her vision would be renewed through a shift to a collegial structure.

I also felt confident in the new leadership models, because in Romania, I experienced leadership that was life-giving and inclusive in the person of Sister Augusta. She was a natural leader, ahead of her time. I took on Sister Augusta's attitudes as the ideal. From the time I arrived in the U.S., Sister Augusta's letters mentored and supported me. She reaffirmed my own aspirations for our Buffalo community, particularly during this period of renewal. She searched for the new definition of our community's identity within the context of Vatican II. In one letter she wrote, "I am reading the *Dutch Catechism*. I wonder why the beauty of our faith and our life were not always taught this way. If they had been, perhaps the world would have been better." And, "I have aged considerably and old age has stripped me of many things; but, thank God, one thing is left: the spirit of aggiornamento continues to live in me." Through my correspondence with Sister Augusta, I felt supported and empowered to continue my commitment in the direction of renewal for our small unit in Buffalo.

Another factor that expanded my courage to keep speaking out for change was living in a country where free expression was part of the fabric of everyday life. Nightly we witnessed on TV the debates over Vietnam, the women's movement and civil rights. I lived in a culture where people were encouraged to speak their truths. Slowly, but persistently and with determination, our small, dedicated group of Sisters spoke to the vision of a new way of living in community. We hoped and prayed that the next Chapter would enable us to realize our dreams. Yet, within the context of all these supports, in my heart I knew it was the individual Sisters in Buffalo who kept me motivated to find a new way.

A Great Disappointment
During these years, some unexpected events happened in my own life.

A problem developed after I returned to my work at Catholic Charities. My new supervisor was not trained in the community organization model, and the more I became involved with this aspect of social work, the more he felt threatened. He did not know how to supervise me in this area, and he became critical of my work. It was very hard for me. I tried to learn from him, and I tried to share what I was thinking, but the exchanges were not productive.

At that time, Catholic Charities hired a highly competent social worker from Rochester, New York who monitored all programs and facilitated the work on every level. He was friendly to me, and I felt he respected me. He even invited me to dinner with his family. We worked together on a neighborhood survey, and he was extremely supportive of me. I would say we became friends. I even consulted with him about dynamics in our community.

He was smart and knowledgeable, but my relationship with him changed when he organized a particular in-service training. At the in-service meeting, he encouraged each person to openly express questions and frustrations. I did just that. With sincerity, I spoke about my difficulties. That proved to be a very big mistake.

The agency could not accept that I did not 100 percent conform to or follow the expectations of my supervisor. Catholic Charities supported my supervisor. Later, I understood that this was the case because my supervisor had been a competent and loyal Catholic Charities employee for a long time.

I talked about what happened with Michael Avanzato, the head of the Community Development Department at Catholic Charities. He gently responded by saying that I would probably do better in another setting. He suggested that I consider teaching.

When I realized I was being let go, I was shocked and deeply hurt. I was trying to find my way in this free world, and to think that two years after I started my first ministry in this country, it ended this way. It was heartbreaking for me.

In retrospect, I realize I was naïve. People do not accept change very easily, and I should have had deeper roots in the agency before trying to introduce new ideas. I tried to give my best, but my best was not what was wanted at that point. I wrote a detailed paper on what happened to explain the situation to the General Council. This was especially difficult to do, because not only was I disappointed, but the Sisters had placed great hopes in my career, and I felt I was a disappointment to them, too.

Chapter Thirteen

"Through this deeper, experiential acceptance, I found a new surrender. In a way, I was healed at Lourdes."

1970-1975

In the summer of 1970, the developments at Catholic Charities coincided with the cancer metastasis to my lung. It was a shock, but at the same time, I knew it could happen. I was soon to face two major surgeries: an adrenalectomy and an ovariectomy. My doctors believed that through these surgeries, my hormonal activities would be eliminated. This seemed the only way I could hope to prevent further metastases.

My doctor made it clear that there was no guarantee the two procedures would save my life. I thought my death was soon to come, and I surrendered. I was not afraid. The Lord, however, would restore me again.

More than ever, through this experience, I found myself celebrating the gift and mystery of my own life. In the light of death, some things seem to lose their importance, whereas others seem to gain greater importance. Love appeared evermore as the most vital aspect of both life and death. God's fidelity was the overwhelming experience of my life.

Yet, there were moments of darkness, doubt, discouragement, and loneliness. Had it depended on me, I probably would not have made it through, but I discovered with greater clarity God's presence in my life. A deep gratitude was born in my heart that led me to ask: "What can I give God in return?"

I wrote my own Magnificat, thanking God for the times of darkness and light, and for the revelations that came to me through both suffering and joy. I celebrated and praised God for all those who communicated God's love to me: my parents, family, and the special prophets who challenged me to greater heights.

The community of my Sisters was a source of life and comfort to me. My many friends became part of this new challenge in my life by sharing in both my sorrow and joy, and by gifting me with their affection, fidelity, trust, loving care, and affirmation.

A New Career: Rosary Hill College

While I was recuperating, I heard of an opening at Rosary Hill College, which is now called Daemen College. In September 1970, I was hired as a part-time instructor, and I taught two sections of "Introduction to Social Work" in the Sociology Department. I never thought I would be a teacher, but I wanted to contribute, and this was an opportunity. I felt grateful to be in a ministry again. This opportunity was a challenge and a new beginning.

The community was concerned it might be too much for me, but when I consulted with Dr. Manzella, he was very encouraging. "Go into it, go into it. It's important for people to have meaning in their lives," he told me. He had no hesitation. That is how I started my seventeen-year career at Daemen College. Every day was a gift to enjoy and give.

For my teaching, I used the social work models I learned at D'Youville College and the University at Buffalo. There were things I liked about teaching, but I did not feel I had a natural inclination to it. I tried very much to involve the students, and I also enjoyed working with individuals. I was interested in developing relationships with my students and sensitizing them to the needs of people. Most of the students came from middle class backgrounds, so it was my great desire to help them learn more about minority groups and poverty.

This aspect of the social work profession was very important to me as a Sister of Social Service. As a community, we are called to work for systemic change and legislative action. Education for social work is an integral part of the spirit and mission of our community's charism. As such, I felt at home with the academic world's values and philosophy, and I liked the constant invitation to learn more. The college experience gave me the opportunity to work with the community at large, and I enjoyed that very much.

The previous summer, I had planned to travel to Romania, but because of the recurrence of my illness, I postponed the trip until the summer after my first year at Daemen. Since I was now a United States citizen, I could include a visit to Eastern Europe.

When Sister Augusta learned of my trip, she requested that I go to Lourdes on my way to Eastern Europe. This was not something I, myself, would have decided to do, but the Sisters in Romania felt strongly that I visit Lourdes. So for them, I went.

Lourdes
Before I visited Lourdes, I went to Paris to see my friends, Annie and

Nora Samuelli, and my teacher from high school, Sister Rodica. It was wonderful to reconnect with these old friends.

When I got to Lourdes, I had to wait in line. As I was waiting, I heard one woman say that although she knew it was not possible for her to be cured, she offered herself for someone else who was ill. She said in offering herself for someone else, much peace was given to her. She felt a deeper healing.

That made sense to me. I thought about this when I entered the baths. In this way, the experience at Lourdes had meaning for me. I did not necessarily believe that God worked miracles in that way for me, but I, too, was willing to offer myself for another. Through this deeper, experiential acceptance, I found a new surrender. In a way, I was healed at Lourdes.

From Lourdes, I flew to Rome for three days, and I tried to see everything. I was terribly tired, but it was a great experience. Then I went on to Bucharest where I spent a few days with Sister Hildegard. We had not seen each other since prison. When I left prison, it broke my heart that she still had eight years left to serve. Fortunately, an amnesty allowed her to leave before her eight years were up. After seeing Sister Hildegard, I visited Sister Augusta and other Sisters in Cluj.

A Reunion in Romania

I spent two weeks in Cluj. I saw Sister Augusta every day and was surrounded by her love. How grateful I was to God, to her, and to all who made it possible for me to visit her for the last time. She died three years later.

My friend, Marika Lengyel, also spent time with me during this visit. Marika is the loving, helpful woman who was a great support to me when I was released from prison and lived in Gherla. I thought this would be my first and last visit because of my cancer's recurrence. We were all so happy to be together. Everyone spoiled me. Who knew I was to return again and again?

New Directions at the College

In the fall of 1971, I returned to Daemen College. Before long, my work became even more challenging. The students taking social work courses initiated the idea of extending the courses, and Dr. Roslyn Gerard, the Sociology Department Head, proposed the establishment of a social work program, and that I be hired full-time to implement the plan. This meant that I, as one faculty person, was responsible for the administration of the entire program, teaching all the courses, arranging the students' field placements, supervising the students, and finding and working with the field placement agencies. The accreditation process was, in itself, another full-time job. I did not find this work at the college glamorous or particularly prestigious. For me it was important work, but work with extraordinary demands.

Eventually, in 1975, a former graduate of Daemen College, Peggy Lenahan, helped me set up an Advisory Board to support the fledgling program. It was a wonderful Board made up of politicians, social workers and community people who believed in social work. I met with individuals and the entire Board. I was given assignments, and I coordinated the Board's various suggestions. We were told that the Social Work Department would be effective only if it were accredited.

The National Association of Social Workers (NASW) encouraged all undergraduate institutions to have their social work programs accredited. A certified program assured sound preparation for graduates. Building the program was too much of a challenge for me alone, so I relied on many people to help me develop an accredited program. With the help of the Board, I prepared and submitted the first self-study for the on-site visit of the certification group.

After our first site visit in May 1976, we were rejected. This was primarily due to the fact that I was the only full-time faculty member, and the accreditation team looked for more than one faculty member as a measure of the program's solidity. As a result of the rejection, the school felt pressured to hire more people.

During the next few years, we followed the certification group's recommendations and hired excellent teachers who taught relevant electives, as well as the core curricula. Karen Schimke, who eventually worked on both county and state levels, was the second full-time faculty member hired. With the help of the Board, we brought in a consultant to guide our decisions. Those years were very stressful. I never imagined my original job would evolve in this way. Teaching my classes, supervising students in their placements, and coordinating the accreditation of the social work program were activities parallel with my leadership responsibilities in my community's renewal.

In 1973, my community celebrated its 50th anniversary. That occasion prompted me to reflect on my own life, as I, too, celebrated my 50th birthday.

I wrote my "Song of Thanksgiving": I thank you God, with all my heart, and praise your name, because of your constant love and faithfulness. (Ps. 138). This was a time of gratitude and hope.

Sister Augusta Ikrich

In 1973, another major event happened. It was the year that Sister Augusta died. She died during the week the Society was preparing to celebrate the Golden Anniversary of its Foundation. She was buried on May 12, 1973. And so it happened that at the time of her death, Sister Augusta, who was so community-minded and who concentrated all her efforts in building unity, brought all the Sisters together. As the Sisters stood around her coffin, they experienced their oneness of mind and heart and were strengthened in their determination to live up to the glorious heritage that Sister Augusta gave them.

At this time in the community, different ways of doing things and/or experimentation was encouraged. As part of the experimentation, the Sisters asked, and were allowed to select, a House Superior by secret ballot. I was elected to this position in 1973.

In January 1974, I also was appointed to the position of General Councilor on the General Council. My first task as a General Councilor was to visit Los Angeles for a Sisters of Social Service Federation meeting from January 28 - February 1, 1975. I was appointed to replace Sister Nicoletta, who had died, and I traveled with Sister Natalie and Sister Suzanne. I was very interested in the Federation, how it had developed and what it meant to our Buffalo community, as well as to the other member groups. I will now provide a brief background on the creation of the Federation.

The Federation: A Brief History

The Federation of the Sisters of Social Service is comprised of three autonomous branches: California, Canada and Buffalo. Each group, while sharing common roots and charism, operates independently and has its own General Council and representatives. Up until 1953, the three branches were one unit; however, in 1953, the Californian branch became autonomous, and then the Canadian branch followed suit a few years later.

The factors contributing to the separation included cultural differences, our Foundress Sister Margaret's deteriorating health and a lack of communication among the Sisters as a result of World War II.

Sister Margaret – having fought the Nazis and Communism, and needing to flee Hungary as the Communists gained more and more control of the country – suffered the aftermath of the role she played in trying to save her homeland from the horrors of both these regimes. In short, she began to age.

During the war years, she often was unable to communicate with the Sisters in America. As such, she was unaware of the developments taking place in the United States. And, when she came to the United States, Sister Margaret was unable to see that the American culture called for different expressions of living out our charism. The styles and expectations of Sister Margaret and the Sisters in America were worlds apart. Both had difficulties accepting these differences, and as a result, the separation occurred. Eventually, the Vatican stepped in and the Federation was formed.

I had great compassion for the confusion experienced by the Californian and Canadian Sisters, because I, too, met a changed Sister Margaret. Shortly after my arrival to the United States in 1964, Sister Natalie took me to Tuxedo Park, New York to greet Sister Margaret. I was looking forward to seeing Sister Margaret again so much, because she played a critical and heroic role in my life and in the lives of the hundreds of Jews she saved. But my visit was very painful. Sister Margaret was not the woman I knew between 1944 and 1947. It took years for me and many others to come to grips with this reality.

By the end of the 1960s, the younger generation of the Californian Sisters began to inquire about their past. This was in part due to Vatican II's calling of religious to return to their origins. Ultimately, this desire to revisit the past and reflect on its impact on the future, spilled over into all three branches.

One of our Californian Sisters, Sister Jean Marie Renfro, was commissioned to research the history of the Sisters of Social Service. She wrote "The path to Federation reflects joy and pain, separating and coming together. It is the common charism, heritage and mission that kept the Sisters faithful and united in spirit throughout the years of separation of various kinds. It is the same charism, heritage and mission that will enable the Sisters to read the signs of the times in the 1990s and into the 21st century, and to be a prophetic voice that needs to be raised wherever the Sisters of Social Service live and work."

I can say with deep gratitude that Sister Jean Marie's words have proved true, as the Sisters of Social Service continue to move forward, together, in this new century. Overall, Sister Jean Marie's words capture the love and hope we eventually experienced as three communities united in one Spirit.

The 1975 Chapter

After I returned from the 1975 Federation meeting, I carried out my usual responsibilities at Daemen College and fulfilled my obligations to the community. I was deeply involved in writing the position paper, "The Biblical Foundation of Our Apostolate" for the 1975 Chapter.

Sister Anne Marie Fitzsimmons, a Mercy Sister in Buffalo, was asked to be our Chapter facilitator. With her help, we developed new processes that guaranteed everyone a voice and ensured the principles of participation would be fully utilized. Sister Anne Marie also kept us focused on our original charism, which was the instruction from the Sacred Congregation and Canon Law.

In 1975, Sister Anne Lehner was elected as General Moderator of all the Sisters of Social Service for a four-year term. I was elected Assistant General Moderator. The Chapter also approved the development of the U.S. District. Soon after the Chapter, the U.S. District membership elected me to be the first U.S. District Moderator. Besides my increasing responsibilities at Daemen, I now held these two new roles. I worried about how I would manage, but the Sisters always encouraged me and promised to help in any way possible. It amazed me that the Sisters felt these leadership roles were easy for me; that was not so. I had to learn to speak in public and do many other things, which at first, I did not feel comfortable doing. I was happy to accept leadership to help our community, but for me it was a situation of learning, being challenged and hoping I would meet the expectations. I lived through much anxiety over my abilities, but the one thing that kept me open to the many challenges was the love and support of my Sisters.

During the 1975 Chapter, we followed the instructions given by the Sacred Congregation. We looked at our original charism, which flowed into our ministry, and tried to define what needed to be changed in light of the times. The decisions were recorded in the document, *Life in the Spirit*, which became our interim Constitution. Every Sister of Social Service received her own copy of the interim Constitution and was asked to give feedback to the General Council. There was satisfaction that significant work was accomplished at the Chapter. We took great risks distributing the material to our Sisters living underground, as I will explain in later chapters.

Challenges in Leadership

With my community and professional responsibilities, I felt the pressure of leadership that necessitated splitting my time and energy in many different areas. My challenge was to do the best job possible in each of my roles.

During 1975 and in the following years, I felt the important thing for me to do was to serve the Sisters in the U.S. District. Earlier, many of the Sisters hoped they would someday return to Eastern Europe, but as Communism entrenched itself more deeply, we realized our challenge was to find ways to live out our charism in America. It took a great deal of time to plan and implement programs so that our Sisters in the U.S. District could be exposed to the new vision of religious life.

The spirit of "Aggiornamento," which means updating or renewal, called us to search out ways we could internalize the new vision of religious life in light of the needs of the times, as well as fully embrace the needs and aspirations of a new country. Our Council did everything to bring a new way of living to our community through collegiality.

As mentioned earlier, one of the most demanding tasks of the General Leadership at that time was to rewrite the community's Constitution in the spirit of Vatican II. We did the rewriting in Buffalo and sent it to all our Districts throughout the world for feedback.

Many of the Districts, especially those under Communist rule, read it without any concept of the new theology of Vatican II. They returned our work, and we had to agree on revisions and corrections. This was an extraordinary task. I did some of the work, along with Sisters Teresina and Angela, but Sister Anne handled the majority of the revisions.

Our need for a new Constitution was something the Sisters in Europe could not understand. Furthermore, it was written in the Post-Vatican style, which was pastoral and spiritual, not legalistic. Sister Anne and I experienced challenging times during visitations when European Sisters shared their dissatisfaction with the Constitution. It was very difficult for both them and us.

We placed great value on the visitations to our Districts that were under Communist rule; however, it took a lot of time and energy to explore, plan and go on the trips. I made the visitations and enjoyed being with the Sisters, but it was extremely demanding.

Chapter Fourteen

"I came to recognize the times of darkness as experiencing in a new way God's love for me."

1975-1978

The 1975 Chapter had just taken place, and a beautiful energy and spirit-filled momentum from the meeting permeated the air. In the years to follow, I experienced the most intense work of my life in my roles as Assistant General Moderator, U.S. District Moderator, representative to the Federation of the Sisters of Social Service, and my jobs as Department Head and faculty member at Daemen College. I was called to leadership in many ways.

It was a privilege to work on the General Council with Sister Anne and Sister Angela. We were of one mind and one heart for bringing about renewal. It was our hope to serve our Sisters so they could respond to the needs of the people in our time and place. Moreover, we wanted to make a contribution to the American Church and to the larger society around us.

For our ministry of leadership, we had to establish a new, participatory and collegial model mandated by the Church. Also, we wanted to realize community among ourselves, share faith, call each other to grow, and have an area of responsibility for each Sister in which she would creatively contribute to guiding the total community. We divided up the areas of responsibility among us: Spirituality and Prayer; Ongoing Formation and Care of the Elderly; and, where I focused my energy – Ministry and Social Justice.

We established a number of objectives for ourselves in our roles as leaders. We wanted to provide each Sister in every District the experience of knowing she is our greatest asset and gift. We worked to create a climate that would deepen our sense of unity. We encouraged the Districts to concentrate on the areas of prayer, community and government, and to set up a process to evaluate the progress in these areas. We explored new ways of deepening our commitment to social justice. We expressed our commitment to enhance human dignity by promoting reverence and adequate care for our elderly Sisters. And, we looked at our overall financial situation, to possibly provide for a more viable arrangement.

It was important to us that each Sister in the community feel supported in her ministry and service. To achieve these goals, we decided to continue some of the traditional ways of support, like the publication of *The Herald*, our source of international news regarding the Sisters of Social Service. We also continued to provide the community with yearly mottoes, which served as common points of meditation, and thereby enhanced our unity.

Visitations to Underground Sisters

Members of the General Council continued their visitations to the Districts in different parts of the world, and engaged in continual group and personal correspondence. We, as Council Members, also participated in and facilitated the District Assemblies in Buffalo, and in those communities suffering under Communist oppression. These assemblies were held biannually for the purpose of reviewing Chapter decisions and formulating District policies. The Sisters under Communism, deprived of spiritual nourishment, appreciated the Council's pastoral leadership, which offered spiritual talks at underground retreats. We also gave individual spiritual direction to our underground Sisters whenever possible.

During the visitations, we all made efforts to deepen our prayer life, and to facilitate ongoing efforts to explore ways we could live out our charism. Our efforts for unity went beyond the boundaries of our Districts to the member communities of the Federation.

At our Federation meeting in Buffalo, held January 2-4, 1977, we committed ourselves to a joint study of our charism, to the social justice implication of our vows, and to the work for a common Constitution to safeguard a common spirituality and heritage.

It was a really exciting time. Sister Anne, Sister Angela and I all felt deeply committed to grow in our roles, along with the commitment to invite the community at large to grow.

During the summer of 1978 (June 1-July 31), in my role as Assistant to the General Moderator, I traveled to Eastern Europe to visit our Sisters. These visits were done with great risk, because the Sisters were still underground and visitors posed a danger.

With a prison record, I was especially suspect. I was extremely careful to leave no thread of religious evidence in my hotel room or on my person. We brought little written material and the Sisters often memorized any spiritual or communal information we shared so as not to jeopardize themselves or others.

Sister Anne, Sister Angela and I were fearful during these visitations, but the courage of the Sisters strengthened our resolve to support them in any way possible. Our goal was to update them in new theology and share in their struggles. We made ourselves available to them at any time or place.

During the visits with our underground Sisters, I often reflected back on the last twenty five years. In 1950, more than 10,000 religious members were deported from their convents to holding camps. As a result, many orders left Eastern Europe, or thinking the suppression would be short-lived, disbanded. In our tradition of resistance, the Sisters of Social Service went underground. In Romania, we played a leading role in the Catholic Resistance Movement, which lasted from 1950 to 1989, until the fall of the Berlin Wall.

Our Sisters' decision to continue as a religious community was done at tremendous cost. If a Sister was found out, she was interrogated, threatened, and quite possibly imprisoned, along with her entire family. In fact, between 1950 and 1964, in Romania, fifteen Sisters and three Associate members were sentenced for a total of 142 years. No one felt secure.

At this time, Transylvania was again annexed to Romania, so Romania felt the constant threat of Hungary. Yet, in the midst of this constant tension, our Hungarian Sisters still attempted to communicate with our Romanian Sisters. And, even with this constant fear, many young women still chose to enter our community. They felt called to give their lives to God and the conditions did not deter them; in fact, in some cases, it gave them more determination.

During this time, our Sisters lived two lives, openly working and participating in society, and secretly living their religious lives. The Sisters' health and strength often suffered from the demands of these two forces. After a full day's work, the Sisters met with the poor and sick, secretly visited Catholic homes to encourage parents to educate their children in the tenet of their faith, and planned spiritual and communal gatherings with other Sisters.

The District Moderator in Hungary, Sister Helga Gerstner, organized the Sisters secretly into groups. As a protection, one group did not know of the other groups. Even though the group members were scattered, once a week or so they met covertly to pray, share the vision of their consecrated lives, and support each other with encouragement. Sometimes they helped each other in practical ways, like sharing information on jobs or places to live. Since they were trained for religious ministries, the Sisters found it difficult to obtain work. They lived in constant fear of being discovered.

For me, the visitations were inspiring experiences. I saw how the Sisters maintained relations with one another, and in their great desire to grow in our charism and special mission, took risks by accepting new members. It was an important time for me to share with them our vision, call and way of living in the free world.

Whenever we visited, we were available for individual spiritual advice, as well as for talking with the Sisters and encouraging their continuing efforts. It was frustrating for the Sisters not to participate in the life of the Church or in a ministry. We all had to learn how the "ministry of presence" would be a new way of serving the Church. We also talked with these Sisters about the Constitution and requested their feedback.

Our visits were preceded by extensive consultation with Father Cassian Yuhaus, Director of the Center for Applied Research in the Apostolate (C.A.R.A.) in Washington D.C. Of central importance to the Sisters of Social Service was and is the search for renewal, and for an adequate response to the world of today — whether it be in a socialist system or a capitalist one. My visits to the Communist countries contributed tremendously to my understanding of social, political and economic developments, as well as to the responses to these conditions by the people involved.

In addition to my work with the Sisters underground in Europe and Cuba, at home I sought out organizations that furthered my education on justice. The Center For Justice, Western New York Peace Center, Network, Buffalo Area Metropolitan Ministry, Executive Board of the Sisters' Assembly of the Diocese of Buffalo, and the Social Justice Committee of the Lay Advisory Board all extended my understanding of structural causes of injustice. All these experiences contributed to my preparation for our next Chapter meeting.

The 1979 Chapter in Switzerland

In 1978, we asked Father Cassian Yuhaus to help us prepare for the 1979 Chapter in a totally new way. We arranged for the Chapter to take place in the summer of 1979 at the Ursuline Motherhouse in Sion, Switzerland, rather than in Buffalo. Due to visa problems because of Communism, we realized very few of our Sisters could attend a Chapter in the U.S.

Father Cassian supplied us with a program structure that incorporated the Sisters of Social Service's history and charism. The extensive program was entitled, "Theology of Vocation and Religious Life in an Age of Change and Renewal." This comprehensive program gave our whole community a sense of where we were called to be.

At the Chapter, Sister Anne was re-elected General Moderator, I was re-elected to be her Assistant, and Sister Angela was re-elected as Councilor. My position's term was six years in length, from 1979 to 1985.

After the Chapter, I also was re-elected as U.S. District Moderator for a three year term. Having realized Father Cassian's great gifts and abilities, I asked him to help us with the District development. He came to Buffalo and we organized a number of workshops. As an entire District, we worked intensively on internalizing the current thinking on religious life in light of Vatican II, as well as the new understanding of theology in these changing times.

Father Cassian was instrumental in helping us see how precious our charism was. He helped us understand our role as Sisters of Social Service in the Church, post Vatican II, in the United States.

These were years of great intensity where, nourished by new insights and energy, we implemented the plan and made it a reality. It was a turning point for our community; great hope and a common vision were restored.

However, on a personal level, in my second term as Assistant Moderator, I realized I could not keep working for both the District and the Generalate due to the enormous responsibility required by both positions.

My five jobs, Chairperson and faculty member of the Social Work Program at Daemen College, Assistant General Moderator to Sister Anne, representative to the Federation, and U.S. District Moderator, with responsibilities to serve the Sisters in Buffalo and throughout our District, all took their toll on me.

Chapter Fifteen

"The Holy Spirit has worked among us and has united us."

1980-1983
Self Renewal

Sensing my need to be energized, I actively looked for ways I could be renewed. Since I had a great desire to understand more about the global situation, I attended a seminar on "Inequality and Contemporary Revolutions" at the University of Michigan at Ann Arbor, from June - August 1980. The seminar was sponsored by the National Endowment for the Humanities.

The question of inequality in its various forms – human rights, human dignity, social justice, and global interdependence – raised issues of deep personal concern. Additionally, I saw how information gained from this seminar could be used to engage my students in an active search for a more just and humane society.

Overall, the seminar enabled me to fulfill more effectively my role as social work educator, and it provided me with new stimulation. I hoped that a deeper understanding of the forces determining our foreign policy and a clearer vision of the factors shaping a new world order would be a source of hope not only for myself, but also for my students, and for everyone they, in turn, would serve. In addition, I shared the insights I gained at the seminar with my religious community, as well as with a wider circle of friends and associates.

In September 1980, after a great deal of inner struggle, I asked to be excused from my responsibilities as the Assistant General Moderator. Sister Anne and Sister Angela did not accept my resignation, but instead granted me a leave of absence for one year, effective immediately.

At that same time, I also took an unpaid leave of absence from Daemen College for the fall semester, as I was totally exhausted. My need for renewal and my leave made it possible for me to participate in the Guelph Program at Loyola House in Ontario, Canada. The program consisted of a thirty-day Ignatian retreat, which was followed by ten days of lectures and discussions. The focus of these lectures and discussions was to gain a deeper understanding of what the retreat meant to us, in addition to receiving insights for spiritual direction.

It was a most needed respite after all my years of activity and work involvement. I longed for a time of real solitude, and the retreat gave me this opportunity. It was a wonderful time of grace when I realized how God's love manifested throughout my whole life. I came to recognize times of darkness as experiencing, in a new way, God's love for me.

I was able to accept my limitations and forgive myself for my failures and mistakes. One special and significant message I received was the realization that we, as human beings, are not God, and that we must constantly remind ourselves not to expect of ourselves more than what God expects of us. It was a time of physical and emotional renewal that I sorely needed.

Return to Duties

I returned to my faculty and Program Director duties at Daemen in January 1981. The social work program underwent a second mandatory review at this time and was reaccredited. I was proud to be part of that success.

Spirituality

In July 1981, I requested and was granted an extension of my leave of absence from the position of Assistant Moderator at the Generalate level. At this time, my energies were focused on preparing for the U.S. District Assembly meeting.

In August 1981, we held the U.S. District Assembly meeting in Buffalo, and we were fortunate to have Father Cassian with us again. He ended a homily with these encouraging words: "The Sisters of Social Service have a very important role in the Church of today and tomorrow – to show the Church and the world that you desire with all your hearts to work for a better world."

At the Assembly, I was asked to share what the renewal meant to me. I said, for me, it meant, "to continue the mission of Jesus, our call is to challenge the world, and the structures that keep people down and oppress them, so they cannot actualize themselves. Remember there is personal sin and social sin. We are called to address both. In this lies the tremendous greatness of our vocation. Before, there was more concern with individual sin, but Sister Margaret recognized there was another kind of sin. In the life of Jesus, we see a concern about what happens in the world. We can never be grateful enough for our inheritance, which we share in common.

"In our struggle to clarify our vision, the Lord calls us to understand the fullness of our call and to embrace all that the Lord has given us: the diversity of gifts and the diversity of ministries. The Sisters of Social Service will never be in one ministry only. As Sisters, we each represent a segment of our charism, and together we live it out in its fullness. No one can fully live it out alone.

"I have come to a deeper gratitude for my own call and for the call of the Sisters of Social Service – and I have now an even greater desire to build the future: God's kingdom of love. Thank you for being instrumental in this. I have grown by being with you. I cannot really tell you how much I was inspired and challenged by each of you. I cannot tell you how much my understanding, warmth, affection, respect, and appreciation for all of you have grown.

"The Holy Spirit has worked among us and has united us. He has given us His grace to be ready to go out as apostles and minister to others while being together with Him. We are united in the Spirit. We are mutually supportive in implementing the decisions of the Assembly. In summary, this time for me was an experience of grace, inner growth, renewed understanding and appreciation for my vocation, renewed appreciation for all of you, my Sisters, and renewed understanding and appreciation of our call. It has brought me a new sense of Joy and new sense of Hope!"

By 1982, preparations for the 1985 Chapter meeting were underway. It was an intense period for me and for all the Sisters of Social Service. Our 1979 Chapter mandated that we have a Constitution Committee to continue revisions. And, based on feedback received at the 1979 Chapter, we established a Post Chapter International Constitution Commission. It was a time of intense work for all the Sisters on the Commission. Sister Anne and I attended a Constitution meeting in Sion during the summer of 1982. The purpose of this meeting was to assess again the Constitution and clarify the issues raised by our Sisters. The result of the Commission's three years of work was the Revised Constitution of 1982. This work formed part of the preparation for the 1985 Chapter.

In February 1983, my term as District Moderator came to an end. From 1975 to 1983, my work energies were focused primarily on the U.S. District. After February 1983, I resumed my work with the Generalate and helped Sister Anne more with these duties. We continued preparing for the 1985 Chapter.

A Visit to Eastern Europe and Remembering Family
    In the summer of 1983, in my capacity as Assistant to the General

Moderator, I undertook an extended visitation to the Eastern European countries where our Sisters continued to live underground. My trip began in Budapest with a visit to my Uncle Alexander's widow, Irene. After Uncle Alexander (my mother's brother) died, Irene became an important link for me to the family I lost so many years before. My visits with Irene brought back many memories of the war.

After the war, I went to Budapest to spend time with Alexander, Irene and my cousin, Evelyn. Uncle Alexander loved my mother and sisters very much, so when we came together, we shared memories and we grieved. We also grieved the tragic deaths of Uncle Alexander's brother Geza's daughter, Lily, and her family. I, too, was heartbroken when I learned about Lily's death.

I remembered Lily with great affection. When I was in high school, she came to Salonta to intern as a pharmacist with my father. Lily was the kind of person who brought lightness and joy to everyone. She eventually married, and she and her husband, George, had two sons.

It was in August 1944 when Lily suffered her tragic fate. At that time, Soviet troops were heading to Transylvania, and everyone was afraid of falling into the Soviet's hands. To avoid being captured, George and Lily made plans to escape. However, when their contact did not arrive the day they were to leave, George panicked. Fearing the fate his family might face, he killed Lily and the children, and then committed suicide. My Uncle Geza, a former Ambassador to Yugoslavia, was living under the protection of the Swiss government at the time this happened. He learned of the tragedy through a Swiss newspaper, and he and his wife were devastated by the loss of their beloved daughter and her family. Soon after learning the terrible news, Uncle Geza died of a broken heart. I was in prison when Uncle Geza died.

Throughout the years, I continued to visit Aunt Irene whenever there was an opportunity. It helped to stay with her, both so I could visit with her, and to protect the identity of any other Sisters I would have stayed with during the continued time of Communism.

Another of my father's brothers, Uncle Emeric, emigrated to Australia, and somehow heard that I survived the war. When the war ended, he tried to locate me. He put an ad in the paper requesting anyone contact him if they knew of my whereabouts. He wanted me to be part of his family, and he asked me to move to Australia so he could adopt me. It was a shocking request. Neither a move to Australia nor adoption felt right to me. I was committed to my vocation and even though Sister Augusta suggested that I go and start a community in Australia, I did not feel drawn to do so.

In 1983, after a five-day stay in Budapest, I traveled to Romania and spent time in Cluj, Brasov and Salonta, my hometown, where I renewed acquaintances and checked out the circumstances of my family home. In Romania, from May 30 to June 20, I met with almost every Sister in secret, including the old and the young. Their spirits were very, very beautiful, but it was painful to see how they continued to suffer from the religious and economic situation in Romania.

At this time, Ceausescu was in power and the Communists tightly controlled the country with their politics of terror. There was great poverty, with no end in sight. In Brasov, a large city at the foot of the Carpathian Mountains, I stayed with my brother-in-law, Alexander Gyôri.

Alexander and my sister, Marianne, married soon after Marianne completed high school. My parents would have preferred Marianne meet someone closer to her own age and values, but she and Alexander were in love.

After they married, times were difficult. Alexander's family's business was shut down, and Alexander was sent to a labor camp. Marianne visited him whenever she could. While he was in the labor camp, the Jewish people of our town were deported, including Marianne, who was nine months pregnant with their child. Alexander never saw her again. He survived by somehow escaping from the Nazis who marched his camp members west, most likely to their deaths. Alexander visited me after the war and when I was released from prison. I learned that he, too, was jailed on minor charges during my internment. He eventually remarried, but it was not a happy union and this saddened me. Alexander idealized Marianne to the point of naming his daughter from his second marriage Marianne.

These memories of my family caused me to explore the possibility of going to Poland to visit Auschwitz, almost forty years after my family's deaths. The District Moderator of Hungary wanted to make sure I did not make this trip by myself. Therefore, Sister Kriszta, with whom I was in the novitiate, was asked to accompany me. We went to Poland from July 18 – 22 after I spent nearly a month in Hungary. I was very grateful that Sister Julianna, the Provincial of the Felician Sisters in Buffalo, established contact with the Felician Sisters in Poland, and arranged that I stay with them. When I arrived in Poland, a Felician Sister took us to Auschwitz.

Auschwitz

For many years, I carried in my heart the desire to make a pilgrimage to Auschwitz. I wanted to be connected more deeply to the experiences my loved ones endured in that place — to walk where they walked, to suffer what they suffered. My pilgrimage was an attempt to honor the sufferings and deaths of the four million victims who experienced that horror.

I can find no words to express my feelings. The horror of Auschwitz is so overwhelming that words lose their power. I spent the day in silence — surrounded by ashes scattered on the field. The inhumanity reflected in Auschwitz spoke to me of the immensity and depth of human suffering. I felt I was in a bottomless ocean of suffering, as I thought of the people who had been here. An awe for the martyrdom of the people came over me. How could they have endured this?

As I walked through the different stages, from the place of the "selection process" to the gas chambers, I ached, wondering what this must have meant to my loved ones — my mother, my sisters, Marianne and Marta, and my grandmother. My family and so many others experienced all kinds of deaths, and died in horrific ways. My deep sorrow called up the question, "Where is God?" Yet, I knew in my heart that this horror was not in vain. I had no explanation, yet I believed new life would come out of this. It was a day never to be forgotten.

Later, the Felician Sisters took me on the Czestochowa pilgrimage to the Black Madonna. During this visit, I learned more about the Polish people's oppression.

From Poland, I traveled to Frankfurt and to Freiburg, Germany to visit some of the Sisters from the Transylvania District. From Freiburg, I went to Paris, where I reconnected with the Samuelli sisters.

While in Paris, I traveled by train to Taize for two days. Taize is a wonderful ecumenical center where young people gather to pray and worship. This trip made a great impression on me, as I never saw so many young people from all over the world gathered together to share and pray. Other Sisters from Hungary told me how inspiring this experience was; to participate in it firsthand was a deep confirmation of their reports.

Also during my trip to Paris, I visited my great mentor and former teacher, Sister Rodica, a Sister of Our Lady of Sion. Sister Rodica also taught my sisters, Marianne and Marta, and she and I remained in contact through the time of her departure from Romania after the Communist suppression. It was a great joy to be with her again and to learn about her ministry. It was wonderful to experience her continued openness to all God-seekers. She was bright and compassionate, and did anything to help her former pupils. She shared with me how the Sisters of Sion revisited their mission in light of a totally new understanding of Jewish-Christian relations that developed after Vatican II. It was an inspiration to me to learn of these developments.

Chapter Sixteen

"How can we live out our lives more consciously and deeply, responding to the realities in which we live?"

1984-1987

Preparation for the 1985 Chapter

Once home in Buffalo, I continued my full-time work at Daemen College. During this time, I also was involved in preparing for the 1985 Chapter. This meeting took place in August 1985, and was held in Bühl/Baden, Germany. Unfortunately, the same situation existed as previously in regard to visas. Our Sisters from the Eastern Block could obtain visas for Europe but not the United States.

Our major resource person for the 1985 Chapter meeting was Reverend Walbert Buhlmann, OFM. He gave excellent lectures, which were full of powerful insights on "The Church on Her Way to Year 2000," "Community Constitution Work," "Healthy Tensions in Finding Your Own Identity," and "St. Francis, Prophet."

The 1985 Chapter approved our revised Constitution and charged the new General Council with its promulgation. This meant editing and distributing the Constitution to all Districts under the same difficult circumstances as previously mentioned, especially concerning the Districts behind the Iron Curtain.

An Unexpected Role

It was at this Chapter meeting that I was elected General Moderator. I never could have predicted that I would be the General Moderator, which was a very large responsibility in my eyes. It was humbling that the Sisters found me worthy of this position. I looked at it as a wonderful opportunity to share my vision with the Sisters and to contribute to the understanding and fullness of our life and living out our charism. I always had a profound desire to deepen the spiritual aspects within my community and myself. It was a constant in my life.

I spent much time thinking, reading and reflecting on the question "How can we live out our lives more consciously and deeply, responding to the realities in which we live?" I shared this idea with the Sisters in Buffalo, who sometimes were discouraged because of their lack of success in the American culture. Our new Council desired to address our local needs, as well as the challenges for the Sisters living under oppressive governments.

One of my first responsibilities as General Moderator was a visit to Puerto Rico during my semester break, from December 31, 1985 through January 11, 1986. As a Council, we saw the need for more frequent visitations to all the Districts, and we were able to accomplish sixteen visits between the years 1986 and 1991.

Retirement from One Ministry

When I was elected General Moderator, I naively thought I could continue with my work at Daemen College. Within a matter of months, I realized it was impossible to do justice to both full-time positions, and I asked for a one-year, unpaid leave-of-absence from Daemen College to be effective as of September 1986.

During my leave, the Sisters of Social Service and I tried to figure out how to deal with my two full-time positions. In the end, we decided it would be best for me to resign from Daemen College. I submitted my resignation to be effective as of September 1987.

While I treasured my work, and valued the students, the development the Social Work program and the opportunity to do the ministry that was so close to my heart and to the mission of the Sisters of Social Service, it was now a relief to give it up. My leaving was made easier by the fact that a wonderful person, Karen Little, who continues to this day to be an excellent faculty member, took over my position. I also felt a sense of peace, because I did everything I could, and I did not let the program down. The Social Work Program was fully accredited.

Programs To Strengthen Unity

As the new General Council, we understood our primary ministry was to provide unity within our Society. We felt responsible to encourage, inspire and challenge members to work toward and live in fidelity to our charism and Constitution. We developed many programs as we went along, because most were recent responses to present community needs. As Council members, we found ourselves always asking, "What would help?"

The proceedings of the 1985 Chapter set clear directions for us as we began our term, and as the highest authority, we worked diligently to implement the Chapter decisions. We put everything on a Vatican II foundation. This was not an easy task. Some Sisters thought we didn't need renewal because we already had a modern community, but new ideas still needed to be dealt with. There existed a constant tension between those two factions – those in favor of renewal and those opposed. The Chapters played an important role in our dialogue.

Three meetings with District Moderators were planned and undertaken, with two taking place in Bühl, in 1987 and 1989, and one in Cuba in 1990. During the meetings, moderators from each District attended workshops on Leadership Development, Spiritual Direction, Women's Issues, Nonviolence, Contemporary Interpretation of Vows, Ecclesial Spirit, and Chapter Preparation. Programs for the District Councils also were planned, and they were facilitated by Sister Anne and me in Cuba, Hungary, Romania, and Slovakia between 1986 and 1990. Numerous other enrichment programs were planned and given to different groups of Sisters.

A Time of Intense Traveling

In 1987, I spent one month in Cuba. It was an enriching experience. While I depended on our Cuban Sisters who also knew English to translate for me, I learned more about the Cuban Sisters' language and history, and all they suffered under Communism. I learned of their great determination to live out the charism of the Sisters of Social Service. I felt fortunate to spend time with Sisters individually and as a group, talking about spiritual matters and our lives.

In May 1987, I attended the Federation meeting held in California. In the summer of 1987, I spent the second half of June in Romania, all of July in Hungary and part of August in Slovakia. In these three Districts, I set up enrichment programs for Sisters who were unable to attend our programs in Bühl/Baden, Germany that summer.

The traveling was rigorous during these months and years, but our great desire to help our Sisters living underground absorb and incorporate the renewal theology of religious life made it more than worthwhile. Yet, teaching the theology of renewal was a difficult task, since it called for a different approach to living our charism, and because it had to be understood in the context of very different cultures.

Chapter Seventeen

"The theme for our Chapter: Reclaiming Our Prophetic Call To Be a Transforming Presence in the World."

1987-1991

Cuernavaca

After I was elected General Moderator, and during my 1987 visit to Cuba, I decided it was important to develop further my Spanish so I could communicate first-hand with our Hispanic Sisters. An opportunity for me to learn more Spanish came in 1988 through a program in Cuernavaca, Mexico. Two Sisters of the Los Angeles group, Sister Constance Gregory, who had lived with us in Buffalo, and Sister Ellen Hunter, planned our participation in the "IDEAL" program in Cuernavaca. IDEAL stood for Instituto de Estudios de America Latina, and the program lasted from February to March.

This was the first time I was in Mexico, and it was a very special, beautiful experience. I flew into Guadalajara, and before traveling to Cuernavaca, I visited Zacapu, where a small community of Sisters of Social Service lived. I was happy to see their house in Zacapu and to learn about their ministry. I could only stay a few days, but the Sisters took me to see the surrounding areas.

From Zacapu, I traveled by bus to Cuernavaca, where I studied Spanish for five weeks. It was an excellent program. Participants stayed with Mexican families, and it was a wonderful experience to share meals and speak in Spanish. As part of the program, we visited Taxco, Mexico City and the pyramids at Teotihuacan. I was fascinated by the whole experience.

I came home from Mexico with the resolve to keep up my language studies and further develop them. In the fall of 1988, I enrolled in an advanced course at Canisius College in Buffalo. I enjoyed the course very much, but during this time, I suffered another medical set-back.

Medical Realities

In November 1988, after a calm Saturday of writing correspondence, I went for a walk, as was my habit, to mail my letters before 5:00 p.m. After posting the letters, I realized I could not continue walking because I could not breathe well. I sat down on the steps of a nearby funeral home and wondered if I was having a heart attack.

A kind woman who worked at the funeral home saw me sitting there and came out to ask if I needed help, and if she should call an ambulance. I said yes and asked the ambulance drivers to take me to Sisters Hospital. Unfortunately, the emergency room was quite busy with a major trauma.

I did not feel pain, but rather a sense of peace as I waited to speak to the doctors. The doctors confirmed that I had had a heart attack. I received a new drug that was proven to help, but it became clear that the damage to my heart muscle was significant. Still, the doctors felt that my condition could best be handled with medication. My rehabilitation proceeded slowly. I attended the cardiac rehabilitation sessions, but it was months before I felt well.

To give me time to rehabilitate, Sister Anne took over my duties as General Moderator. It was not easy for Sister Anne, because by now she was not only Assistant to the General Moderator, she also was District Moderator for the United States. To ease Sister Anne's load, Sister Angela helped out with many of my responsibilities.

The Liberation of Eastern Europe: Preparation

The years of 1989, 1990 and 1991 were very intense, as so much needed attention, especially in the Eastern European countries. In 1989, the great liberation of Eastern Europe took place when the Berlin Wall fell and the Eastern European countries were freed from Communist regimes. This greatly affected the Sisters of Social Service because Eastern Europe was where our community was founded and where most of our Sisters lived. We felt in deep solidarity with our Eastern European Sisters, whose new freedom meant they were legally re-established after a long period of suppression and living underground. Transition from Communism to freedom, however, was not a smooth process. All of a sudden, a new era began in the European Sisters' lives.

During my last year as General Moderator, from the summer of 1990 to the summer of 1991, Sister Anne and I visited all the Districts. We went to Hungary, Romania and Slovakia, and, on a separate visit, to Cuba to assess the different communities and the individual Sisters. We gave talks during the visitations and also explored discussion topics for our upcoming 1991 Chapter. These were very special visitations and preparation times, since we looked forward to openly meeting for the first time since 1948 in

Budapest, Hungary, the birthplace of our Society. We knew we had to talk with the Eastern European Sisters about how their new freedom would affect their religious lives, as well as about how to reclaim our original charism.

Planning for the 1991 Chapter was a great challenge, considering the changes that came about in the countries where our membership lived. I was grateful that with the dedication of my Council, Sister Anne, Sister Ottilia and Sister Angela, we could respond to our Sisters' needs, and I could continue in my General Moderator role.

The Chapter of 1991 was particularly significant for several reasons. After so many years, full representation of all our Districts was possible again. Also, as the winds of freedom blew over the countries of Eastern Europe, we offered new opportunities for shaping a more just and humane future.

The theme of our Chapter expressed the context in which we wished to address the Chapter agenda, "Reclaiming Our Prophetic Call To Be a Transforming Presence in the World." Deep in our hearts were the questions: "Where is God calling us?" and "How can we make real the promises of the new opportunities?"

An interview I gave to the local newspaper in Buffalo expressed the critical moment we experienced: "We are at a unique moment in history, a time of tremendous opportunities for shaping the future. For the first time in 43 years, representatives from all our five Districts: the United States, Cuba, Hungary, Slovakia, and Romania, will come together to reassess our mission and to explore new ways of meeting the ever-changing pastoral needs of the people of God. The Chapter will give the Sisters of Eastern Europe the type of empowering experience and joyful hope they need to begin their challenging work for the Church. The unprecedented changes in Eastern Europe since 1989 have tremendously impacted the Sisters. With freedom after so many years of suppression comes an enormous need to evangelize and rebuild."

Our letter to the Chapter delegates further expressed my concerns and hopes. "While we rejoice, we at the same time grieve. We feel all the pain and anxiety that are being experienced in this transition: the insecurity, the confusion, even the hopelessness of many people. The old system is gone, but the new system has not yet taken deep root. Dealing with the devastation that Communism has left behind is a great challenge. The challenge is really not only with our words and works, but with our lives, to give witness to the Gospel in a world that has been deeply affected by atheistic philosophy. This is a time when we are called to become the Gospel, the good news, and are challenged to make the message credible."

The transition challenged the Council to be acutely aware of the Eastern European Sisters' apprehensions and concerns as they bridged their lives from an oppressive regime to a situation of new-found freedom. Sister Anne was extremely important to me during this time. She was healthier than I, and therefore could deal much better with any issues regarding the 1991 Chapter. I really could not do very much because I was so tired and in pain from the angina, but I still wanted to figure out how I could contribute.

The Chapter of 1991

On Pentecost Sunday, July 7, 1991, I gave the opening address for the 11th General Chapter in Hungary. I tried to find the words to express the mystery and wonder that were present that day. "I turn to you dear Sisters, to all of you who are present, and to all our Sisters everywhere who are not here physically, but who are present in spirit and love. You have carried the vision in your hearts. You allowed the Spirit to shape in you the image of Christ. You have been light in darkness to each other and to the people around you... The new paradigm calls for balance between individual rights and community needs...the core of the new paradigm is prophetic interdependence, and prophetic interdependence requires ongoing transformation.

"The emerging paradigm begins with saying, 'I don't know who I am.' The Self is a mystery, part of creation. Life is an ongoing process of discovery. There is a need for integration of mind-body-spirit in a continuous process toward greater wholeness... you are a seed, a silent promise. The future belongs to those who give the next generation a reason to HOPE. We wish to reclaim our prophetic call. We need to be transformed, to embrace the vision, and to become bearers of hope."

Over forty years had passed since our Sisters in the Communist block publicly witnessed their vocation as religious women. The 1991 Chapter saw Sisters of Social Service, who, for many years secretly lived out their calling, now openly join their Sisters from democratic countries to reclaim as one community their common mission and shared charism. It was a time for each of us to discover and reclaim each other. Our past experiences were mysterious and cause for wonderment. The question in the hearts of our Sisters who lived in free countries was, "What was it like to live a religious life without the gift of community living and the public support of the Church?" The Sisters who courageously endured religious life underground asked, "What does it mean for a religious woman to experience 'the open window' of Vatican II and the freedoms of democracy?"

Even those who spoke a common language had to learn a new vocabulary, and more importantly, a new way of listening. For both groups of Sisters the reality was a shock. The Sisters from the Eastern European countries struggled to absorb in three weeks time what took the rest of us twenty-five years to process.

We reflected, prayed and worked to our fullest ability to prepare for this historic Chapter. Foremost in our hearts and minds were our Sisters who so valiantly lived out their vocation underground. In our great desire to bring the most current, comprehensive message to them and to the entire Society, the General Council invited the well-known American Benedictine writer and speaker, Sister Joan Chittister, to lead four days of the Chapter. Sister Joan's talks focused on religious life, mission and ministry, the integration of contemplation and action, social sin, and the prophetic call of women religious.

Unfortunately, these talks, which we hoped would be a common foundation for the Chapter, turned out to be an unsettling experience for many Sisters. Although some accepted the message and resonated with Sister Joan, many Sisters could not identify with her ideas. During the years of suppression, we, in America, tried very hard to communicate the ideas of the new theology as best we could, but our underground Sisters were cut off from the many resources and experiences we in the States enjoyed. Unwittingly, we offered years of our own gradual and reflective study to these Sisters, who for more than forty years, sacrificed their very lives to safeguard the Church's teachings. The Eastern European Sisters felt their way of thinking was threatened. In hindsight, we realized that four days was too little time for sharing ideas that we in the free world took for granted.

Sister Joan had spent countless hours preparing the most up-to-date material with great hope to deepen the Sisters' understanding of the spirit of post-Vatican II. However, neither side was prepared for the other's view. I, personally, had agonized over our choice of topics with Sister Joan. And, although we wanted to share the richness of Vatican II's message, we realized the message was too much, too soon. This pained our committee and me. Despite this disappointment, in my heart, I was convinced that as different as our pasts were, we were unified in our charism and our desire to rebuild our community.

On the whole, the Chapter proved to be very successful. On some days, nearly 200 Sisters gathered together to pray and learn. Participants included observers from the Californian and Canadian member groups of the Federation. We greatly appreciated their supportive presence. We also were thankful to have Sister Margaret Collins, SSJ, attend as a facilitator. It was very apparent that our Eastern European Sisters were eager to be open. Overall, the Chapter was held under unique circumstances, and in a unique moment in history. Today, I still give thanks for all that happened during that Chapter.

Because she was so familiar with our community and helped us in many ways, especially with our Constitution, we invited my dear friend, Sister Margaret Mary Bradley from Maryknoll, to join us for the last few days of the Chapter. After the Chapter, she and I visited Oradea and Cluj. Sister Margaret Mary was able to see first hand many of the places where people and events had shaped my life.

After the Chapter, we had many issues to handle because of the drastic changes in the former Communist countries. For instance, the Communists confiscated our original Motherhouse in Budapest and used it for apartments. We now worked at reclaiming the building, which was in very poor shape. It took us years to settle the property issue, and we ended up choosing compensation rather than repossession, because to have made repairs to the building would have cost much more than what the property was worth.

The new era was fraught with ambiguity and complications. The change in the political climate was extremely problematic because many Communists stayed in power and people felt that the revolution was stolen from them. In so many ways, our Sisters in Eastern Europe, like other citizens, found only a partial freedom after the fall of the Berlin Wall.

Chapter Eighteen

"God's vision of our mission is one that must take shape in a modern form."

1991

Before and after the 1991 Chapter, I experienced serious health problems, which will be discussed in the next chapter, but here I would like to share a paper I gave at the Elms College Institute in Chicopee, Massachusetts in the summer of 1992. The theme of the Institute was "Women Called To Prophecy." Preparation for the Institute gave me an opportunity to reflect on the significance of our historic 1991 Chapter.

Sister Mary Dooley, SSJ, explained the theme of the Institute in her invitational letter, "As we approach the threshold of a new millennium, we believe that this topic is most relevant for women religious and associates. Indeed, as Patricia Wittberg, SC, writes in *Creating a Future for Religious Life*, 'It is time again for sowing, for rebirth, for growth.' In order to carry out our theme we hope to develop a theological appreciation for our prophetic legacy in the scriptures; listen more deeply to the prophetic voice within each of us; broaden our understanding of the prophetic experience of our Sisters in countries in Eastern Europe; experience the prophetic life of a church of the people; and join with our associates in exploring prophetic possibility…"

The first part of my presentation was an overview of my early life. It was based primarily on the oral history I was working on with Joan Albarella. The second part of my presentation specifically addressed the Chapter of 1991's theme, "Reclaiming Our Prophetic Call." My presentation sums up the prophet's call and emotions shared at the conclusion of the Chapter.

"For most of us, the last forty years have been like a wandering in the desert – living in anonymity, yet giving witness by a ministry of presence. With the new freedom given to us, we felt God's call – we were to recover our great gift, the prophetic call, which was so marvelously reflected in the life of our Foundress and of our founding members. Sister Margaret was able to confront the world she lived in with the Gospel message. She was ready to risk everything, even her own life, in order to denounce the injustices and promote alternatives that would reflect Gospel values.

"As Sisters of Social Service, we felt we were bound to the continuity of our charism. In our hearts was the burning desire to search for new ways, for creative ways, to respond to the demands of our present world. The concrete question we asked ourselves was: 'How can we be a truly prophetic community, one that will convey a truly transforming presence in the world?'

"The words of Sister Margaret echoed in our hearts: 'God's vision of our mission is one that must take shape in a modern form. We are pioneers for a better world, working for social reform, not through decrees imposed by power but through renewal of the spirit from within.' We all knew God called us to a new beginning… We all knew that in order to be a transforming presence to the world, we, both as individuals, and as community, needed to be transformed. We were to allow the Spirit to create in us a new heart, a new spirit.

"The moment of the opening of the Chapter is unforgettable. As 180 of us gathered, we all were filled with amazement, wonder, gratitude and joy. We realized God's faithfulness to us. We felt like Saint Paul, who said: 'We patiently endured suffering and hardship and trouble of every kind. We have been put in jail, we have faced angry mobs, we worked to exhaustion, we stayed awake through sleepless nights of watching, and we have gone without food. The world ignored us, but we were known to God. We were close to death, but here we are, still very much alive. We have been injured, but kept from death. Sorrowful, though we are always rejoicing. Poor, yet we enrich many. We seem to have nothing, yet everything is ours.' (2 Cor.6: 5-10).

"The years of suffering and persecution have not destroyed us, have not debilitated us. On the contrary, they made us stronger. Our history testifies to God's faithfulness to us. This is a powerful source of energy for us: the Spirit, in whom our lives are centered, held us together, enabled us to give life. The tree of our community grew and produced new branches and new leaves.

"And, as the countries of Eastern Europe move from a Communist system to a market economy, many people may experience dissatisfaction, disappointment and hopelessness. Inflation and rising unemployment may result in the dropping of living standards of average families. Some will get rich, but the masses may become poorer.

"All problems and crises, which the state is unable to solve satisfactorily, are laid on the shoulders of the Church. The Church is aware of its mission to mediate salvation and hope, but at the same time, is overwhelmed by the high expectations placed on it, and the few resources that are available. Many bishops are new to their positions and are inexperienced in governing dioceses. Clergy are few, materials are scarce, and the needs are great.

"Communism is not dead. Former party members are still in many bureaucratic and administrative positions and they continue to create obstacles for the Church (i.e. delays in returning Church properties, not allowing access to broadcasting facilities for religious programming, and controlling the appointment of teachers to university facilities).

"The Church and the religious orders belong to the impoverished layers of society. This helps to create a bond among the Church, the poor and the homeless. Also, in most countries, the Church is credible because it suffered with the people. Many people see the Church as playing a key role in the development of their nations and in assisting the growth of democracy.

"However, the role of the laity is ambiguous. During persecution, both clergy and laity suffer for their faith, keeping the faith alive. The new freedom brings a new problem: some clergy want to return to a more clerically directed Church, and some of the laity are resisting.

"What does it mean to the Sisters to come from underground to freedom? Of course, it means relief from constant fear, and joy over the opportunities to freely associate with other Sisters. For some Sisters, it is an indescribable joy to discover that we have a whole generation of young Sisters. During the oppression, contact between young and old was extremely dangerous, and therefore, almost completely eliminated from their lives.

"Yet, it also is scary! An awesome responsibility exists – now people will expect so much, knowing that we ARE Sisters…our lives and actions will be even more scrutinized, and we will not only account for who we are as persons, but will represent the community. Fear and uncertainty have overcome some of the Sisters.

"It is important at this time to remember that the community always had two kinds of membership. The Sisters needed time to decide. Some have chosen to remain unidentified. Others have opted for the conventual's lifestyle. Related to this also is the question of communal living. Now that this is possible, it seems very few actually desire it. The reality is that for all their committed life, the new generation of members, with few exceptions, lived alone. Today, they do not feel the need to live under the same roof. Their way of life enables them to experience community in other ways, such as weekly meetings, informal contact, etc.

"It also is hard to resist the trend reflected in most traditional communities. Moving in together was immediately promoted, as this was considered essential fifty years ago. However, our young Sisters need to know that in our tradition, things are somewhat different. It is alright to be a Sister in the non-conventional life style.

"There are other areas where our Sisters need to adjust to the new situation. During oppression, accountability was exercised in a certain way. Now, new policies have to be adhered to, which require a more organized and structured way. This, in a way, requires more discipline. Previously no records were kept, out of fear of the secret police. Now this is a necessity. All of this means giving up some of one's own independence, learning new ways of relating and sharing in the community's concerns and projects.

"Many Sisters have the desire to engage in direct service within the structure of the Church. Whereas in the past the majority worked in secular jobs, now they wish to participate in the Church's pastoral work at the parish level. The Church, likewise, looks to the Sisters to respond to the many needs of the people.

"What are some of the difficulties? The Church, being poor, is unable to give a decent salary to its employees. Yet many of our Sisters cannot afford to work on a low stipend because they have financial obligations to their families. A number of our Sisters, however, who can engage in pastoral work, discovered that many clergy have pre-Vatican attitudes with regard to religious women. Whereas the Sisters are respected and recognized in their secular jobs, here they are not accepted as partners in ministry. In some instances, this caused great disappointment. The Sisters need to come to grips with this reality and learn to deal with it. They were not prepared for this.

"Another significant area of concern related to ministry is the lack of professional competence in social work and social service. Our community was the only one in the Communist countries known as having social service as its primary area of ministry. Today, there is a tremendous need for addressing social problems. For forty years, the government claimed there was no need for social services, because the government took care of all the problems. The transition from Communism to Democracy creates many new problems and no one is prepared to deal with them. Our Sisters feel they have a call, but they feel totally unprepared to respond to the need. They never had an education in their field; it just was not available. Now, they are faced with the dilemma of how to prepare our Sisters for this ministry which is so desperately needed and can be freely undertaken, but for which they, themselves, are not prepared!

"Education in areas that relate to our particular charism is a great need. The study of social encyclicals, the preparation for the social mission of the Church, are among our priorities, along with all that relates to religious education and pastoral work. In some instances (e.g. in Hungary), it was possible to study theology over the last ten years. Some of our Sisters availed themselves of these opportunities. However, there is a concern regarding the quality of the training they received – much more is needed in this respect. There also is a scarcity of resource material. It seems it will take a long time to acquire more competence. The motivation for learning and studying is very high, yet the possibilities are quite limited in both social work related areas and in theology.

"While our Sisters did not have opportunities for formal education, they carried in their hearts our vision. They closely followed the political, social and economic development of their country, and tried to evaluate critically the new developments and to discern them in the light of the gospel values. They are deeply aware of the significance of the present moment, when policies for the future are being formed. They know they have an important role to play, not only by direct service to the poor, but by shaping society's direction into the future.

"One of our greatest challenges is how to live out the prophetic role in a pluralistic democratic society. Our Sisters, as the rest of the citizens of these countries, lived a great part of their lives under a totalitarian system. They do not know how to use freedom. They have not experienced a more democratic way, and this is not easily learned, if one did not have such traditions. For forty years, political ministry was not an option. And yet, for our community, political ministry is very important. We believe we are called to participate in the shaping of public policy, on whatever level we may be able to do this.

"How to promote Christian values in a pluralistic society is a great challenge. Some Christians still have the illusion that Christianity is to be totalitarian, as was Communism. There are some who advocate 'restorationism,' a return to the era when Christian influence was exercised from above, as in the monarchical regimes. In the new post-revolutionary setting, convinced believers welcome the opportunities to argue their case in free and open discussion. Granted, there is an important place for religious authority, but in a pluralistic society, any truth must make its own way by open communication and conviction, by argument and not by imposition. Learning how to confront and dialogue with pluralism and ecumenism, and how to continue the work for peace and social justice are great challenges for the Church and for all Christians.

"In our broken, divided world, we are to be a community that reflects the Trinity: unity in diversity. We will be prophetic insofar as we witness with our lives that it is possible to be one, while we are many. In our times, we have seen the extremes of collectivism and individualism. Our community is no exception. We all experience the tension, and yet we know the balance between the two is where unity can be created. Prophetic interdependence is what we must strive for in all our relationships, within community and with the world around us!

"It is our hope that the Spirit will free us, so that we can empower each other and become a community where each individual will participate, according to her giftedness, for the sake of the whole."

Chapter Nineteen

"During the 1990s, my hopes and dreams culminated in many significant events."

1992-1999

In early 1992, I was elected Assistant District Moderator. As such, I focused on what would continue to help our Sisters not only in our District, but in the other Districts, too. Although I was physically weak, Sister Angela, our District Moderator, encouraged me to pursue my interest in spiritual direction through the Saint Joseph Center. My participation at the center allowed me to offer spiritual direction to both religious and lay people. I also provided private and group retreats throughout the 1990s.

And, despite suffering from some serious medical problems in the last decade of the 20th century, I came to see many of my hopes and dreams culminate in numerous positive events: the destruction of the Berlin Wall, the 75th Anniversary of the Foundation of the Sisters of Social Service, the 50th Jubilee of my vows, the renewal of the Federation, and the 50th Anniversary of the Sisters of Social Service in the Diocese of Buffalo. For me, the celebrations meant freedom for my Sisters and new hope for all people.

I probably would not have witnessed all these celebratory events if it were not for my second cousin, Dr. Daniel Domjan, a cardiologist. In the spring of 1991, I got in touch with Daniel, to tell him I would be in Los Angeles in June for the Federation meeting. I hoped to see him and his family. Daniel is the grandson of my Aunt Irene, and son of her daughter, Evelyn, who lives in the States.

As a heart surgeon, Daniel inquired about my condition and convinced me to let him set up a series of examinations to assess my chances of surviving heart surgery. I gratefully accepted his offer and underwent a number of risky tests. The tests revealed that I should pursue open-heart surgery. Daniel encouraged me to have the surgery as soon as possible.

In the summer of 1992, my cardiologist in Buffalo told me I probably would not survive another heart attack, and that open-heart bypass surgery was strongly recommended. Even though Daniel told me the same news a year earlier, the reality of my situation still came as a shock to me. I still thought I would get better with medication. I realized I was at high risk, so after prayers, consultation and a deep process of discernment, which included facing death, I decided to undergo the heart surgery. I wrote good-bye letters to all my friends, and I expressed my total surrender to whatever would happen.

The bypass surgery took place on November 18, 1992 at the Cleveland Clinic, considered to be the best in our region. Prior to going to Cleveland, I visited Dr. Manzella, my surgeon and wonderful friend. He was in the terminal stage of cancer. Neither of us knew how long we would live. As it happened, Dr. Manzella died on the very day I underwent the bypass surgery. I learned of his death one week later. What a mystery, death and life. Dr. Manzella's dying on the very same day I received a new chance to live was extremely meaningful to me. He went and I came back.

Eastern European Sisters Come to Buffalo

While I was recovering, because of my education and experience with students, Sister Anne asked me to be the resource person for the Eastern European Sisters who came to Buffalo for advanced schooling. Some actually decided to emigrate and live in America, while others wanted to take advantage of schooling so they could return and strengthen their devastated countries. Helping these beautiful young Sisters was a joy to me. I remembered coming to this new land with questions and concerns about academic challenges and cultural expectations, so I could identify with their concerns. They made many adjustments to live in a country with vastly different resources and values.

The Sisters came primarily to be educated, and I was happy to assist them with their studies. I mentored them, offered them guidance, and upon request, led directed retreats for them. I was very proud of these Sisters' accomplishments. Because of their sacrifices and determination, they were prepared to return to meet the challenges of Eastern Europe. Their spirit gave me hope for the future of the community.

Renewed Dedication to the Federation

Another great satisfaction for me in the 1990s was the continued dedication of the members of the Federation. From my earliest days in the United States, I always was very interested in the Federation's history and our three groups' mutual interdependence. Now, years later, I witnessed how effort and goodwill brought our diverse groups to a common understanding of our charism. In 1993, the Federation gathering, held at the Center for Renewal at Stella Niagara, New York, proved to be a time of reconciliation and growth. We were challenged to heal the wounds of separation. Trusting our common charism, members of the Federation listened to each other with open hearts. The Sisters shared stories to express their experiences of separation and alienation, and yet also their common mission and vision. This open dialogue strengthened the building of trust and love among us. The Spirit was with us. I had great hope for a strong future.

At this time, we also celebrated our 70th Anniversary as Sisters of Social Service. Sisters came from Mexico, Cuba, Taiwan, Hungary, Slovakia, Romania, Canada, and the United States. This was the largest representation we ever had at the Federation. The gathering began with an anniversary Mass at our parish, Blessed Sacrament Church, in Buffalo.

Then, we convened at the Retreat Center at Stella Niagara. The noted theologian, Monika Hellwig, gave three presentations that focused on the development of theology and the diversity within the Church. We saw how we had grown in our understanding of renewal in our own lives, as well as in the community of the Sisters of Social Service and the community of the Church. Aggiornamento was taking hold. Yet, all the while we worked to strengthen our community in the United States, we were constantly aware of Eastern European Sisters' needs. These Sisters, who suffered under oppression for so many years, continued to adjust to their new lives, and needed exposure not only to the tenets of aggiornamento, but also to education.

Sisters of Social Service Ministries Training Seminar

To address this great need, at the close of the 1993 Federation meeting, the Sisters of Social Service Ministries Training Seminar was held in Hamilton, Ontario, Canada. Sister Anne Field and I were the Steering Committee Coordinators. We presented the seminar to twenty-five Sisters from Hungary, Slovakia, Romania, Cuba, and Mexico, along with twenty-five Sisters from the United States and Canada.

An explanation of the seminar's goals was sent to all Sisters interested in presenting at the seminar. It stated, "The seminar is an effort to share Sisters of Social Service ministerial experience, making connections between this, our charism and our experience of God in our ministry. The objective of the seminar is the facilitation of basic, effective delivery of social services and pastoral care in each participant's country of origin. The seminar specifically has been initiated in response to the request to share our ministerial understandings with our Sisters in Eastern Europe who systematically have been denied access to contemporary means of working with, and on behalf of, the poor and marginal. We hope the seminar also will facilitate future ways of encouraging the laity, with the Sisters, to take initiative in bringing people to a new awareness of their roles as active participants in rebuilding their society."

In the midst of all this, another medical problem occurred. In 1994, the vertebrae in my neck fractured. There was a risk of neurological compromise due to degeneration of the cervical spine fractures. It was a time of very deep discernment because the doctors could not assure me of any success with surgery, however, the alternative was that for the rest of my life, I would be paralyzed. After praying and consulting with the Sisters, I decided to undergo the surgery.

I was in the hospital from May through July 1994, and I had a long recovery after that. The dedication of the Sisters was unbelievable – they were with me day and night, and they supported me with their love.

Social Work Advanced Training Institute

I had a long recuperation, but once I was feeling stronger I contributed to our community's commitment to help our Eastern European Sisters gain an education in social work. One creative approach included the Social Work Advanced Training Institute. The Institute was designed and developed by Dr. Shirley Lord, a Social Work Educator at Buffalo State College, Sister Teresina and me. As part of our program, we put together a series of seminars for our Sisters and others who worked in social work but who were not given an opportunity to acquire a basic background in social work. Dr. Lord wrote a social work manual for the Institute, and it was translated into Hungarian. I was able to help with the translation of the curriculum.

Sister Teresina and Dr. Lord gave the seminar in Hungary and Slovakia, and it proved to be a great success. Sister Teresina helped translate many materials into Hungarian and traveled with Dr. Lord as an interpreter and support person.

To this date, it remains a challenge to contribute to the rebuilding of our European Districts. The Bishops of the United States and the Leadership Conference of Women Religious (LCWR), as well as several religious orders in the United States, have made and continue to make great contributions to support our Sisters in Eastern Europe. We are very grateful for their help.

Fifty Years in Buffalo

In March 1997, we, the Sisters of Social Service in Buffalo, celebrated our 50th year of permanent settlement in the Diocese. On March 4, 1947, three of our Sisters arrived in Buffalo from Hungary.

This anniversary coincided with the 150th Anniversary of the Diocese of Buffalo. In a "Brief Historical Overview" I wrote for the *Western New York Catholic* newspaper, I reflected on the past fifty years: "We have grateful memories of the Carmelites, Sisters of Saint Joseph, the Franciscan Sisters of Stella Niagara, and the Mercy Sisters, whose hospitality and interest sustained us through the immigrants' trials of adjusting to a new land."

I also pointed out that, "before the fall of the Berlin Wall, our Sisters in Buffalo were the only group that had the privilege of living and working in a free society, and they provided leadership for our communities who, though under suppression, continued their 'ministry of presence' to the silent Church in Eastern Europe. The service of leadership also was extended to our Sisters under oppression in Cuba."

1997 Chapter in Kosice

In 1997, I traveled to Kosice, Sloviaka as an Ex-Officio member of the 1997 Chapter. The 1997 Chapter was a great experience that demonstrated all the progress that was made between 1991 and 1997. Sister Anne was re-elected as General Moderator for a second term, and, while I was not well enough to work intensely on any committee, I participated whenever I could. It was great to be able to contribute, even in a limited way.

On the weekends, several trips were organized. It was wonderful to see the beauty of Slovakia and to learn more about the country's history. The Slovakian Sisters were extremely kind and hospitable. They made every effort to accommodate me, knowing that my energies were limited.

After the Chapter, the Sisters had a choice of visiting either Hungary or Romania. I joined the delegates of Cuba who were interested in Romania. While in Oradea, we made a short trip to Salonta, and we visited the cemetery where my father is buried. I am grateful to the Sisters in Oradea who take care of his grave. While in Salonta, we also visited the house where I lived with my family. These were poignant visits.

Next, we went to Miercurea-Ciuc, where we stayed with our younger Sisters, and then we drove to Cluj. It was a joy for me to see, even if for a brief moment, the places that were familiar to me in beautiful Transylvania.

I returned to Buffalo with gratitude for our Society. Although I knew it would take our Eastern European Sisters further great effort and patience to live through the continued transition from their lives under Communism to lives of new freedom, I was sure of their goodness and resolve.

75th Anniversary of the Founding of the Society

The celebration of the 75th Anniversary of the founding of the Society reflected our jubilee motto, "Life giving spirit: Lead us on." In Buffalo, on May 21, 1998, Bishop Henry Mansell presided at our Liturgy of Jubilee at Blessed Sacrament Church. Several historical articles about our community appeared in the local Catholic paper, and in October, our Annual Dinner also celebrated this anniversary.

In an article I wrote about the anniversary, I spoke about our history and the influence of our Foundress, Sister Margaret Slachta: "Her prophetic vision and call for concern and action around political economical issues as a part of Christian spirituality continue to be a challenge. In particular, Sister Margaret is remembered for her openness to the Spirit, for her uncompromising response to the needs of the times, for her prophetic voice to raise political consciousness, and her confidence in women to be responsible agents for shaping the future in the spirit of the gospel."

Sister Melinda Townsend, a member of our Los Angeles Sisters who was pursuing her doctorate at Fordham University, gave the main address at the anniversary dinner. Her presentation was entitled, "Weaving a Tapestry of Hope: Celebrating Seventy-Five Years."

1998 Federation Meeting in Pannonhalma

Another major event I was fortunate to participate in was the 1998 Federation meeting held in August 1998 in Pannonhalma, Hungary. In order to visit friends, I arrived in Eastern Europe before the commencement of the meeting.

When visiting Bucharest, I was shocked by the terrible conditions there. The country had no means for rebuilding. But while I was there I had a beautiful reunion with two friends I met in prison, Antonetta and Olympia Prefit. I stayed with them for a week, and during that time, we met with other friends and shared our experiences.

I continued my travels to Gherla where I visited my friend, Marika Lengyel. It was almost forty years since kind Marika helped me find a place to live in my lonely days after being released from prison. As a political ex-prisoner, I was considered a persona non grata, and the Sisters couldn't let me live with them because they couldn't risk their own imprisonment. I always remembered Marika's great compassion for me in that desolate time. I now found Marika's life to be very difficult and full of increased family responsibilities. Her daughter was not in good health, so Marika tried in every way to support her and help take care of the children. Marika told me how she and so many others in Transylvania had difficulty finding work and providing economically for their families. I was saddened to see how demoralized these strong and resourceful people had become because of so few opportunities and resources. From Marika's home, I went to Cluj and Alba Julia where I visited with the Sisters before going to Salonta.

After visiting Salonta, I went on to Pannonhalma to the Federation meeting. The Federation was a special time, because on August 9, all those present celebrated the 75th Jubilee of our Foundation. Sisters were present from California, Mexico, Canada, Cuba, Romania, Taiwan, Slovakia, the Philippines, Hungary, and Buffalo.

The selection of Pannonhalma was very meaningful because of the history of its Benedictine Monastery. And, the monastery is very significant to the Sisters of Social Service because our Benedictine spirituality is connected to it.

Sister Michele Walsh gave a reflection at the Anniversary Liturgy. In it she expressed, "Today, seventy-five years later, we must turn to each other and acknowledge our mutual interdependence, our common faith in the Spirit of God working with us and in us…let us consciously renew our dedication to our community and to each other."

The goals of the 1998 Federation meeting and Anniversary celebration were best expressed in the *Summary Remarks*: "This…occasion enabled us to focus on our gifts, our strengths and the necessity for us to continue to work for justice as our founding Sisters so beautifully exemplified for us. We left the meetings with the conviction to continue working with each other to address the challenges of globalization in a world that we all must share, nourish and cherish."

After the Federation meeting, I spent a few days with Father George Kis, the priest who protected and hid our group of novices years ago in Romand when we fled the Soviet advance into Transylvania. He was a very important priest for our Society. During the most critical times in the summer of 1944, when Sister Margaret was involved in organizing opportunities for Jewish people to be prepared for baptism, Father Kis generously offered his services. Like me, he came from a Jewish background.

Sharing My Story in California and Mexico

From May 10-18, 1999, although my strength was diminishing from more frequent angina, I was happy to offer a Pre-Pentecost Retreat for thirty nine Sisters of Social Service and Associates in Los Angeles, California. The theme of the retreat was "Sisters of Social Service Charism and Spirituality." Fifteen videos were produced covering most of the retreat presentations.

I explained the general format of the retreat in my introduction: "I thought our retreat should look at our shared history, giving thanks for God's faithfulness to us, and asking ourselves, 'Where does God call us?'

"I thought one way to do this would be by sharing our own stories with each other, listening to one another, discovering a new way to God's presence in our lives – where we came from, where we have been throughout our lives, and where we are today. I believe God was revealed to us and God speaks to us. I will begin by sharing with you my story. Many of you have already heard my story, and I hesitate in doing this. Yet, I have come to see that my story is actually God's gift, God's work in me."

In August 1999, I returned to the West Coast, but this time I went to Zacapu, Mexico, twelve years after my first trip there. I gave a retreat for the Mexican Sisters of Social Service, and since I had been part of the community for so many years, I was asked to share my knowledge of the community's history with those preparing for first profession. They were interested in hearing from someone who had the European experience and had known our Foundress.

When the retreat ended, I participated in the great celebration of the first profession of three Sisters at Tacambaro, a nearby city. All the new Sisters' parents and family attended. My experience in Mexico was deeply satisfying. I am grateful for the warm hospitality and kindness shown by the Mexican Sisters, as well as their great desire to grow as a group to live out their charism.

The Advisory Board for the Buffalo Sisters of Social Service

Back in Buffalo, I continued to work with our Sister students, the infirmed Sisters, and also with our Advisory Board. Our Advisory Board grew and expanded its service to our community during the 1990s. In 1963,

Mr. Gregory Deck organized our Advisory Board at the request of Bishop Burke of Buffalo. The Board had several functions during its history, but its primary purpose is to help us stay rooted in the culture of the United States. Following our tradition and belief in the laity's inclusion in our mission, we welcomed the establishment of a Board. I remember with gratitude those who took on the role of chairpersons. During my term as District Moderator, Mr. Ray Wopperer was the Board's Chairperson. His openness and affirmation of our needs and hopes gave us courage to live out our charism with our own unique spirit.

Since 1967, the board's activities centered on organizing the Annual Dinner for the purpose of social interaction with the larger society, more visibility, justice, education, and fundraising. On many occasions, we invited speakers who addressed contemporary issues and shared their views and values that reflected our own values and hopes for the local and universal Church.

The Advisory Board supported us in our new projects that provided for our growth and resonated with our spirituality, charism and commitment to live out our mission in this country. Friendships developed with these partners of ours. Some of these people, like Jerry Miller and Mary Frances Danner, befriended me during my first years in America. Their shared interest in social work and their faithful concern for my welfare and the well-being of our community were always a source of consolation and joy.

Friendships

Another friendship that has continued from my earliest days in America is my friendship with the Manzella family. Not only have I enjoyed watching Dr. Anthony (Dinny) and Theresa Manzella's children grow up, but I am now enjoying their children's children, the next generation of Manzellas. They have been faithful and generous friends.

Overall, many friendships have sustained me throughout my education and career, and I thank God for them all. I continue to share in the lives of Caryl Fonda, my teacher, and a special colleague, Ruth Stratton, as they have shared in mine. My friend, Margaret Klipfel, also has been very good to me and to all the Sisters in Buffalo; she can never do enough for us.

In these later years, I have been inspired by the marriage of my friends, Evelyn and Hugh Brady, and I thank God for their faithful concern and love for me. Plus, the many, many beautiful Sisters in the Buffalo area, the Benedictines in Erie, PA, and my beloved Sisters in the Maryknoll community in Ossining, NY, have continually reaffirmed my own vision of, and commitment to, religious life. And, although on the other side of this large land, the Los Angeles Sisters of Social Service always have been close to me through our common history, ideals and friendships. Sister Constance and Sister Michelle in particular supported my vision through their encouragement. I also received support from our Canadian Sisters, especially from Sister Gabriella.

Jim and Audrey Mang of the W.N.Y. Peace Center are friends who challenged me to stand for the tenets of justice, and I am deeply grateful for my friendship with them. I am grateful, too, for new friends like Lisa Monagle, Carol Bagos and Carol Weissert, whose loving generosity have brightened many days.

The End of the Decade and A New Home

The last months of the last decade of the 20th century were unique, as I prepared to move out of the only home I ever knew in the United States. I lived for thirty-six years, from 1964-1999, at 440 Linwood Avenue, Buffalo, New York without any interruption. Yet, with our aging population of Sisters, we knew we had to sell the Linwood property. I was deeply touched by the gentleness with which the District Council handled this process. The Council wanted to make sure that our new arrangements would be adequate, considering the limitations of our age, and every other aspect related to housing, including safety and proximity to other Sisters' houses.

Sister Timea and I, who shared an apartment above the garage of the Linwood house for many years, were interviewed regarding our preferences and the kind of place and circumstances we would favor. First, we considered moving into subsidized housing, but then we were encouraged by the Council to consider moving into a single, one-floor residence. We found an ideal house in Kenmore, a first-ring suburb of Buffalo. We moved in on October 4, 1999.

During this time, many people asked us how we felt about giving up our Linwood home and moving to a smaller house. We knew it was impractical to keep the lovely Victorian property with its many rooms and three floors. And, since we recognized we all needed more manageable housing, it made the decision to leave easier. I was grateful for all the help I received from the Sisters and friends who contributed by sorting, packing, moving, painting, and the final settling in to our new residence. It did not take long for us to feel at home. We both enjoy the house and give thanks for it.

Over the years, many times I have reflected on the "move" of my loved ones from their homes. They were forcibly removed and had to leave everything behind, as they were allowed to only carry a few items. Their hearts must have been filled with anguish, since there was no other home prepared for them. Again, I was thankful for my new opportunity. In fact, my change of residence was a significant event to mark the close of the 1990s that were so full of blessings and hope. I looked forward to future times in my new home.

Epilogue

I find myself, at age seventy-nine, coming full circle to my beginnings: my family and the life-long exploration of the Jewish-Christian struggle.

Many years have passed since the day my loved ones were snatched away from me. Initially, I was unable to find out what happened to them. I carried them in my heart, and I grieved and cried.

Over the last forty years, I have viewed much of the Holocaust documentation, and I have learned a great deal about the atrocities, inhumanity and terrible anguish the Jewish people endured while in the hands of the Nazis. It is beyond any imagination.

In October 1992, I discovered the American Red Cross had set up a Holocaust and War Victims Tracing and Information Center. I initiated the tracing inquiry process to find any information on my mother, two sisters and grandmother.

Four years later, on March 13, 1996, I received a letter from the Holocaust and War Victims Tracing and Information Center (see copy of letter in center of book) stating that my mother was transferred on August 14, 1944 from the Auschwitz Concentration Camp to the Stutthof Concentration Camp, where she died on December 19, 1944. My little sister, Marta, also was transferred to the same camp on August 14, 1944; she died there on January 14, 1945. In some additional information sent by the Red Cross, I read that Stutthof was liberated on May 9, 1945, less than four months after Marta's death.

In March 1998, I received copies of the Nazi's summarized forms, but they contained no further information on the causes of death, just my mother and Marta's prisoner numbers. No information was ever found on my Grandmother or older sister, Marianne, who was in her last month of pregnancy at the time of deportation. During the war, I heard rumors about what happened to prisoners once they arrived at camp. One of those rumors was that the Nazis immediately earmarked any elderly and pregnant women for immediate extermination. That may explain why no information exists on my grandmother and Marianne.

As I continued searching, I discovered terrible things about both Auschwitz and Stutthof. Among all the Nazi camps, Stutthof was nicknamed the "extermination" camp, suggesting it was one of the worst and most brutal. Situated in northern Poland not far from Russia, Stutthof was known for harsh camp conditions, extreme weather and ruthless labor requirements. All these factors led to the quick deaths of prisoners who were not immediately exterminated.

I also read how large transports of Jewish people, mostly women (the majority of them Hungarian) were transferred to Stutthof from Auschwitz in 1944; given the Tracing Center information, I knew my mother and Marta were among them. I read further that of the 50,000 Jewish people brought to Stutthof, nearly all died. Those who had not died by January 1945 were marched westward in dreadful winter conditions, wearing no shoes and only their prison uniforms. Thousands of Jewish people were reported to have perished in the Death Marches, while many other Jewish people, evacuated by sea in small boats, were reported to have drowned in the icy northern waters off Poland.

The attempt to understand the whole experience of the Holocaust, or the Shoah, has been a life-long process for me. While I appreciated the gift of life I was given, I kept asking myself, "How did all this happen?" In the end, there is no answer. I have read about, and sought to understand, the relationship between Judaism and Christianity. I realize that when I converted to Catholicism, I knew little about 2,000 years of hostility between the Catholic Church and the Jewish people. Since then, I learned about the root cause of this hostility, and my heart broke.

We, as Christians, have caused great suffering for the Jews with the popular teaching of supersessionism, or the belief by many Christians that their religion is the "fulfillment" of Judaism, and therefore superior. Especially hurtful has been the focus on deicide. Until recently, the Catholic Church worked toward the conversion of all Jews, praying they be rescued from their darkness and lack of faith.

Mary Boys writes, "Our history would have been radically different if we could have seen that God's relationship with one tradition does not diminish the sacredness of the other's."

A newer image of Jews and Christians as partners in witness and work is reversing two thousand years of Church teaching and popular religious stereotyping. There also is a growing understanding that God loves different people equally. John Paul II, in the first papal visit to the Synagogue of Rome since the time of Saint Peter, said, "As Christians and Jews, following the example of the faith of Abraham, we are called to be a blessing for the world. It is therefore necessary for us, Christians and Jews, to first be a blessing to one another."

When I was twenty-one, I experienced the spirit of Sister Margaret and the Sisters of Social Service, and saw how many of the members lived out their call during the Holocaust; it was a tremendous gift to be part of a group willing to lay down their lives to help Jewish people escape persecution. In honor of this work, and the thousands of lives saved because of it, Sister Margaret was honored as a "Righteous Gentile" by Yad Vashem, the Holocaust Martyrs' and Heroes' Remembrance Authority. She was given a medal inscribed with "If one person can save one life, she has saved the whole world." A tree also was planted in her name in the Holocaust Garden.

Sister Sarah Salkahazi, Sister of Social Service, who also rescued Hungarian Jews in the 1940s, was remembered by our community at our 1999 Annual Dinner. In December 1944, she was executed by the Nazis, along with the Jewish refugees she attempted to shelter and to whom she was devoted. Sister Kay MacDonald, NDS, former Superior General of the Sisters of Our Lady of Sion, was the guest speaker for this dinner. Her speech, entitled "Church and Synagogue: From Historical Rupture to Mutual Relations" challenged us to think about Catholic-Jewish relations in this way:

"If we do not pursue the teaching of the Church with regard to seeking reconciliation and a new relationship with the Jewish people with whom we have such close bonds in Jesus and Holy Scripture, in liturgy and theology, what will be our history with Muslims and Sikhs, Buddhists and Hindus, and Native peoples among whom we live today?"

My heart also resonates with the words written by Edith Stein's niece, Suzanne Balzdorff, in the book *At The Fountain of Elijah: The Carmelite Tradition*:

"Understanding can never be achieved by glossing over or by one side trying to convince the other that it alone is in possession of the truth. Too much pain and suffering have occurred over the centuries... How much better to listen to our brother's cry, to strive for the empathy that my aunt wrote about... to search for ways to help each other, to see the common humanity and grant to others the right to follow the path of their choice by which they reach our common goals.

"Some time ago, we commemorated the 50th anniversary of Kristallnacht, the Night of Broken Glass, November 9-10, 1938. It was the opening of the violent phase of the Holocaust, the pogrom in which synagogues were destroyed and people were arrested and shipped to concentration camps by the thousands. We commemorate, we mourn, but we must stand together and vow to be more sensitive in the future to the cry of human beings, to refuse to join the howling mob, to heal and rescue rather than cast stones and firebrands, and to fight injustice wherever we may find it. That is a goal worth fighting for; that is a purpose to which we can all dedicate ourselves, regardless of race, colour or creed."

Balzdorff's words are especially meaningful to me. In fact, today, I feel the same way as I did as a young woman. After all my reading and searching, I am a Jewish person who is Catholic, living my life, hoping in some way to contribute towards a better future for humanity, a future with justice for all. I ask, "What will bring us together?"

With William Johnson, author of *Arise, My Love...: Mysticism for a New Era*, I rejoice in the signs of hope, in the coming of a new spring. He writes of the hunger for spiritual experience, the search for mysticism, the martyrdom for social justice, the solicitude for the underprivileged, the compassion for the suffering. He says, "In a world torn by violence and strife, priority must be given to the task of reconciliation. Beyond the movement toward reconciliation between Jews and Christians, there is an appeal for dialogue between East and West: As there is no love of God without love of neighbor, so there is no conversion to God without conversion to the world."

Traditionally, in our community, every new Sister chooses a motto that expresses her own hope, her own aspiration — her own vision of her call and mission. I chose: Live on in me, as I do in you... (John 15:4). Jesus' words reflect the unforgettable experience of my discovery of His love; they set me on fire. I had but one longing — that I would respond to that love with my whole life... For me, "Live on in me..." means that I was invited to love in union with LOVE — that Love would be the most important driving desire in all I do, in all that I am.

I envisioned my call and mission as an ongoing journey in which I would strive to reflect and radiate God's love and God's compassion — that I would be a sign, a presence of God's infinite, all-embracing Love in the world.

Deep down in my heart, I felt this dream could only come true through the Spirit dwelling in me. I went through many stages during my years in the community of the Sisters of Social Service. The Spirit within me constantly challenged me to stay awake, and to recognize the countless ways in which Love was revealed to me. I remember these ways with gratitude.

I remember...

The moments of "awakenings," for the invaluable gift of seeing beyond the immediate around me, for being able to trust in God's unconditional love, and for being called to proclaim in my life and death that God is faithful, and God's love is everlasting. It is my fervent wish that I stay awake, and continue to recognize the Spirit's promptings and respond to them...

The moments of ecstasy when I experienced the grandeur and the majesty of the natural world...

The moments when I experienced the depth of love human beings can feel for one another... their readiness to lay down their lives for others...

The moments when I was touched by a human person's strength of ongoing fidelity...

My own moments when I was able to accept forgiveness and bestow it...

The moments when I experienced courage to hear the claim of conscience and follow its deep impulses even in the face of danger...

The moments when the senseless suffering of millions enabled me to hope against hope...

Even in the midst of horror and affliction, God was present to me as Infinite Love, the source of goodness. In my heart, I felt the compassion of God for all suffering people. It was this inner certainty of God's love that sustained me and enabled me to live on. I discovered that death and pain are present in the whole of creation, and that dying is built into life. All this is something that can't be explained...it is a mystery.

I learned to recognize the presence of the Spirit, not only in my life, but everywhere. By continuing my journey with the Spirit dwelling in me, my terrible sense of discouragement is changed into new hope for a new life.

I know God's love for all of us lasts forever.

Bibliography

Many authors have nurtured and sustained me. I could never acknowledge all the writers whose works have been sources of inspiration for me. Yet, some that have had a profound influence on my life are Teilhard de Chardin, Victor Frankl, Thomas Merton, Mahatma Gandhi, Abraham J. Heschel, Thomas Barry, Henry Nouwen, Elizabeth Johnson, Richard Rohr, Joan Chittister, and medieval women mystics.

WORKS CITED

Boys, M. (2000). *Has God Only One Blessing: Judaism as a Source of Christian Self-Understanding*. New York: Paulist Press.

Johnston, W. (2000). *Arise My Love...: Mysticism for a New Era*. Maryknoll: Orbis Books.

McGreal, W. (1999). *At the Fountain of Elijah: The Carmelite Tradition*. Maryknoll: Orbis Books.

Chronology

Dates	Personal History	World History
June 8, 1923	Born Judith Fenyvesi in Salonta, Romania. Daughter of Elizabeth and Francis, sister of Marianne and Marta.	Fascism spreading throughout Europe. Influence of Nazism under Hitler increasing in many countries, including Hungary and Romania.
Sept. 1937	Began studies at the School of the Sisters of Notre Dame de Sion in Oradea.	
Nov. 19, 1938	Baptized Catholic with mother and two sisters.	
1941	Graduated from high school. Enrolled in the School of Social Work of the Sisters of Social Service in Cluj.	1940 - Northern Transylvania annexed to Hungary.
March 1942	Father's death.	1940-1944 - Discrimination against the Jewish people reflected in new restrictive laws introduced in Hungary.
Sept. 1942	Graduated from the School of Social Work.	
Oct. 1942	Began Social Work with the Diocesan Diaspora Office in Cluj.	
May 1944	Employment terminated because of the drastic anti-Jewish laws, including the wearing of yellow stars, ghettoes and deportations.	March 21, 1944 - Nazi Army entered Hungary. Persecution of the Jewish people reaches its climax.
	Received into the Community of the Sisters of Social Service of the Transylvanian Province who offered protection from Nazi persecution.	
	Sister Augusta, Provincial of the Transylvanian Province, took the risk on behalf of all the Sisters and offered life in a gesture of total selflessness and generosity.	May-June 1944 - Jewish people forcibly removed from their homes, placed in ghettoes, and subsequently deported.
	Moved to the novitiate in Oradea in order to be safe.	
1944	First meeting with Sister Margaret Slachta, Foundress of the Sisters of Social Service. Slachta embodied an uncompromising stance in the face of anti-Jewish measures of this era, and inspired all Sisters of Social Service to live out Christ's commandment of love, even at the cost of one's own life.	

Attempts made to rescue mother and sisters were
to no avail.

June 8,   Mother, sisters and grandmother taken to Oradea
1944   ghetto. Saw mother for the last time in the ghetto.

June 27,   Deportation of grandmother, mother and two
1944   sisters. (Later learned that they were taken to
             Auschwitz, where grandmother and pregnant
             older sister were immediately separated and never
             seen again. Mother and younger sister were
             reported seen at other work camps.)

July 1944   Moved from Oradea to novitiate in Szegvar with   August 24, 1944 -
             other Transylvanian novices.   Romania surrenders
                                                                     and joins forces with
Sept.   Szegvar evacuated because of approaching   invading Russians.
1944   Russian army.   An estimated
                                                                     200,000 Hungarians
Oct.   Fourteen first-year novices and two novice   in Northern
1944   directors, after several weeks of moving from   Transylvania killed,
             place to place, housed by Father George Kis in   imprisoned, tortured,
             rectory of his parish in Romand, village in   and/or deported to
             Western Hungary.   forced labor camps.

                                                                     Winter 1944 -
                                                                     Budapest under
March   Russians reach Romand. Everyone living in terror   siege by Russian
25, 1945   because of raping and pillaging.   Army. German
                                                                     Army retreats west.

                                                                     May 7, 1945 -
June   Transylvanian novices asked by the Provincial to   Germany surrenders.
1945   return to Romania.   End of the war
                                                                     declared.

1945 -   Spent the second and third year of the novitiate in
1946   Cluj, because the novitiate in Oradea had been   Northern
             destroyed in the bombing.   Transylvania
                                                                     returned to Romania
                                                                     by Stalin. Borders
                                                                     closed between
                                                                     Romania and
                                                                     Hungary.

Feb.   Four novices illegally cross the border to prepare
1947   for first profession of vows in Budapest.
                                                                     1945-1947 - Stalinist
                                                                     national policies
May 25,   Profession of vows at Pentecost in Budapest with   introduced into the
1947   novices of Hungarian Province.   country.

Summer 1947	Assigned to join the Sisters in Bucharest. Began ministry as Pastoral Assistant in St. Joseph's Cathedral Parish. Worked with Monsignor Joseph Schubert. Through Sister Hildegard, who worked for Catholic Relief Services, a relationship with Nunciature established. Sisters asked to be link between persecuted and suppressed bishops and priests and the Nunciature.	1947-King of Romania abdicates and flees the country. People's Republic of Romania proclaimed. Sister Margaret Slachta again elected to Hungarian Parliament, now Communist controlled. She struggled repeatedly for a government based on Christian principles and values. (Between 1946 and 1948, she addressed Parliament 22 times.) 1948 - Concordat with Vatican revoked. December 1948 - Greek Catholic Church outlawed. 1948-1949 - Decrees passed subordinating the Church to the State. Schools confiscated, charitable enterprises forbidden, and religious orders suppressed. Bishops and vicars arrested.
1949	Began carrying communiqués between bishops and Nunciature.	Attempts made by government to set up so-called National Catholic Church. August 15, 1949 - Police officials go to all convents. Sisters loaded on boxcars for unknown destinations.
Summer 1950	Secret Police awaken Judith and the other Sisters in middle of the night and search apartment in Bucharest.	

	Judith and other Sisters live in fear and terror of police for next several months, yet continue to carry communiques.	All religious communities dissolved and property confiscated.
	Many people connected with Nunciature and/or who participated in Catholic Resistance Movement arrested.	June 1950 - Pastor of St. Joseph's Cathedral Parish, Monsignor Schubert, secretly ordained bishop.
April 23, 1951	Three Sisters arrested: Hildegard, Christine and Judith.	July 1950 - Nuncio charged with espionage and expelled.
1951 - 1952	Systematic interrogations and sentencing of all those involved in the Catholic Resistance Movement.	
	"Show trial," lasting eight days, gave government opportunity to prove that bishops, priests and religious members were spies who worked against the best interests of the working class by siding with capitalist countries.	
	Sister Hildegard sentenced to 18 years. Sister Christine sentenced to 12 years. Sister Dorothea sentenced to 10 years. Judith sentenced to 10 years.	
April 23, 1961	Judith released from prison.	
1961 - 1963	Subjected to numerous hardships because of status as ex-political prisoner: no housing, employment or visa, and restricted permission for settlement.	
1963	Ransomed by Nuncio due to intervention of two ex-political prisoners (Annie and Nora Samuelli) who had made it to the West.	U.S. Civil Rights Movement.
Jan. 21, 1964	Arrived in the United States of America after five months in Vienna, Austria.	April 1964 - Rev. Martin Luther King Jr. assassinated.
	Joined the Sisters of Social Service in Buffalo, NY.	"War on Poverty," Women's Movement, School Desegregation, Vietnam War Protests.
1964 - 1966	Studied at D'Youville College, wrote about prison/communist experiences and the liquidation of religious communities. Discovered writings of Teilhard de Chardin and Victor Frankl.	

146

1966 - 1967	Attended Master's program in Social Work at SUNY Buffalo via Catholic Charities scholarship. First year of field placement at Urban League – deeply identified with minorities.
Feb. 1967	Breast cancer diagnosis and mastectomy. Search for SSS mission in U.S./role of Church with regard to poor and minorities.
Fall 1967	Second year of field work at Commodore Perry Projects.
Summer 1968	Graduated from Master's program. Hired by Catholic Charities as social worker.
May 1969	Research visit to NYC for development of action- oriented youth group in Buffalo.
July 3, 1969	Became U.S. Citizen.
Aug. 1969	Participated in 1969 Chapter of the SSS in Buffalo as delegate of Romanian District.
Summer 1970	Cancer metastasis to lungs. Two surgeries and resignation from Catholic Charities.
Sept. 1970	Began work as part-time instructor of social work at Rosary Hill/Daemen College in Sociology Dept.
Summer 1971	First visit to Europe since arrival in U.S.: Paris, Lourdes, Rome, Bucharest, and Cluj.
Sept. 1971	Daemen students urge development of full Social Work program. Responsible for development and full-time instruction.
1972 - 1975	Full-time instructor and Field Coordinator at Daemen College.
1973 - 1975	House Superior of Linwood Community in Buffalo.
1974	Appointed to General Council.
Jan. - Feb. 1975	First visit to Sisters in Los Angeles. Participated in Federation Meeting there.

Aug. 1975	Chapter held in Buffalo. Approved establishment of U.S. District. Elected Assistant General Moderator for 4-year term. Visitation to Puerto Rico.
Nov. 1975	Elected U.S. District Moderator for 4-year term.
1975 - 1983	Director of Social Work Program at Daemen College.
Summer 1978	Visitation to Eastern European Sisters.
Aug. 1979	Participated in Chapter in Sion, Switzerland.
Fall 1979	Re-elected U.S. District Moderator for 3-year term.
June - Aug. 1980	Received scholarship to attend NEH Seminar on Inequality and Contemporary Revolutions at University of Michigan at Ann Arbor.
Sept. 1980	Leave of absence from Assistant General Moderator duties. Unpaid leave from Daemen College. Attended 40-day Renewal at Loyola House in Guelph, Canada.
Jan. 1981	Resumed Program Director/faculty duties at Daemen College. Program accredited after second review.
Aug. 1981	U.S. District Assembly Meeting in Buffalo.
Summer 1982	Constitution meeting in Sion, Switzerland.

Ceausescu in power.

Feb. 1983	District Moderator term ends. Resumed work with Generalate. Prepared for 1985 Chapter.
May - July 1983	Extended visitation to "underground" Hungarian and Romanian Sisters.
July 1983	Trip to Auschwitz, Poland.
Aug. 1985	Participated in Chapter in Bühl/Baden, Germany. Elected General Moderator for 6-year term.
May 4, 1986	Guest of Jewish Federation of Greater Buffalo; Participated in Righteous Gentile Award for Sister Margaret Slachta.

148